THE POT
AND HOW TO
USE IT

Other Books by Roger Ebert
An Illini Century
A Kiss Is Still a Kiss
Two Weeks in the Midday Sun: A Cannes Notebook
Behind the Phantom's Mask
Roger Ebert's Little Movie Glossary
Roger Ebert's Movie Home Companion
(annually 1986–1993)
Roger Ebert's Video Companion
(annually 1994–1998)
Roger Ebert's Movie Yearbook
(annually 1999–2007, 2009–2010)
Questions for the Movie Answer Man
Roger Ebert's Book of Film: An Anthology
Ebert's Bigger Little Movie Glossary
I Hated, Hated, Hated This Movie
The Great Movies
The Great Movies II
The Great Movies III
Your Movie Sucks
Roger Ebert's Four-Star Reviews—1967–2007
Awake in the Dark: The Best of Roger Ebert
Scorsese by Ebert

With Daniel Curley
The Perfect London Walk

With Gene Siskel
The Future of the Movies: Interviews with Martin Scorsese,
Steven Spielberg, and George Lucas

DVD Commentary Tracks
Citizen Kane
Dark City
Casablanca
Floating Weeds
Crumb
Beyond the Valley of the Dolls

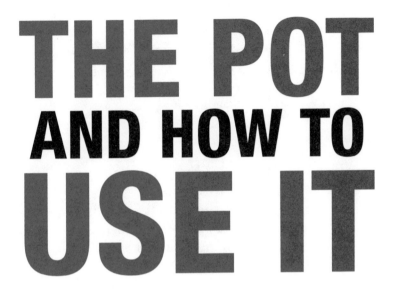

THE POT
AND HOW TO
USE IT

the *mystery* and *romance*
of the *rice cooker*

ROGER EBERT

**Andrews McMeel
Publishing, LLC**
Kansas City • Sydney • London

This book is for Martha, Mary, and Annabel
Three sisters who would find lots wrong with it.

Andrews McMeel Publishing, LLC
an Andrews McMeel Universal company
1130 Walnut Street, Kansas City, Missouri 64106

ISBN: 978-0-7407-9142-0

10 11 12 13 14 RR2 10 9 8 7 6 5 4 3 2

Library of Congress Control Number: 2010921938

www.andrewsmcmeel.com
www.rogerebert.suntimes.com

ATTENTION: SCHOOLS AND BUSINESSES
Andrews McMeel books are available at quantity discounts with bulk purchase for educational, business, or sales promotional use. For information, please e-mail the Andrews McMeel Publishing Special Sales Department:
specialsales@amuniversal.com

CONTENTS

FOREWORD

I love Roger Ebert because he loves life. He loves good movies, he loves his devoted wife, Chaz, he loves all the wonderful folks in his blogosphere, and he loves good food.

And Roger really knows what good food is all about. I am not just talking about what tastes good, but about good food that is healthy and nutritious, too. Roger worked at gaining this knowledge. For many years, he has been an avid participant in the Pritikin Program and a regular attendee at health and fitness resorts such as the one where I work, Rancho La Puerta. At such facilities, he not only learned about healthy food, but also the importance of regular movement, and he applied these principles in his daily life. Most folks will remember that at one time Roger was a bit on the pudgy side. He lost an extraordinary amount of weight the old-fashioned way—by controlling what he put in his mouth and by burning excess calories with regular exercise. He got himself a pedometer, and instead of walking the recommended ten thousand steps per day, he walked twenty thousand. And despite a very sedentary job watching six hours of movies a day, and sitting for many hours thereafter to write his reviews, he lost somewhere in the neighborhood of one hundred pounds. At that point, Roger was absolutely swimming in his clothes. I suggested that he needed a new wardrobe and he replied, "Just a few more pounds." Roger was totally unconcerned about appearances and what others thought. He just wanted to reach his goal.

It was shortly after his incredible weight-loss achievement, that the life that Roger loves threw him a curveball that whacked him, and very hard at that. Roger once confided in me that it miffed him that most folks thought he lost all that weight because of his illness. I am here to testify as an eyewitness that he worked his fanny off by self-discipline and by making profound lifestyle changes.

That Roger should be tested with ill health just goes to show that in life, just as in the movies, the outcomes are not always fair or just. Good people, even when they do so much that is right and healthy, don't always emerge unscathed. I love Roger because, in spite of his challenges, he still loves life, and he still loves good food, even though he cannot eat it. I write this foreword as Roger has just come out of the "cancer closet." In a touching and very revealing article in *Esquire* magazine, he told the world that he could not eat but by the aid of a stomach tube, nor could he speak without a computer-generated voice. A short time later, Roger demonstrated his new computer voice on a segment of *The Oprah Show*. Chaz was in tears as his real voice, pieced together from his many TV appearances, spoke through his laptop to her. There is no doubt that many readers and viewers were as touched by the sweet courage and persistence of this wonderful man as I was and am.

So, I must say that it is an honor to work with Roger on the Pot project. It is Roger's goal to offer you nutritious, satisfying recipes that are relatively quick and easy to prepare and don't stress the system the way modern manufactured foods do and without demanding too much of your precious time. The idea of one-pot meals welcoming hardworking folks with delightful aromas and a promise of a delicious home-cooked meal as they enter the door has enormous appeal for me. What a wonderful greeting after a hard day's work to have dinner in the Pot ready to serve.

Roger mentions the dangers of saturated fat in his text. This is wise caution because hard fats tend to glom on to cholesterol, and together with calcium and sodium form cement that can clog the arteries. But there are some dissenting voices out there about tropical oils such as coconut and palm oil. After all, native folks in the tropics use these fats and have for millennia. These oils can withstand high temperatures and rarely, if ever, go rancid. There is also a move back to butter and lard. Why? Because the alternatives, hydrogenated vegetable shortening and the margarines made from it, are full of toxic trans fats that are one of the leading causes of inflammation and insulin resistance (a.k.a. prediabetes). These free radical bombardier fats are so injurious that cities such as New York and several states have banned them in restaurant food. I am happy to report that none of the recipes in the Pot use these tortured fats.

While on the subject of fat, because Anna Thomas says that the Pot only has two heat levels, "insanely high and barely warm," please use oils that can tolerate the high-heat part. Good choices are monounsaturated fats such as olive oil and high oleic/high-heat sunflower, safflower oil and canola oils (these are hybridized to have more of the properties of olive oil), and peanut oil. Also, consider the more esoteric (and expensive) almond oil, macadamia oil, and avocado oil. Don't use corn, soy, nonhybridized sunflower, safflower, sesame, pumpkin, flax, or any generic "vegetable oils" in high-heat cooking. Any oil that contains substantial amounts of omega-3 (linolenic) or omega-6 (linoleic) fats burn very readily and create toxic chemicals called polycyclic aromatic hydrocarbons (PAHs) and 4-hydroxy-trans-2-nonenal (NHEs). If you want to understand more about what oils tolerate the highest heat, go to www.cookingforengineers.com/article/50/Smoke-Points-of-Various-Fats.

What is a good diet? The experts don't agree. Author Michael Pollan solves the conundrum in his delightful book *In Defense of Food*. He says we live in an "age of nutritionism" where experts have been having some high-echelon food fights. He suggests that the best way to navigate the conflicting food philosophies is to reduce it all to a few overarching principles. In one statement he boils it all down to perfect simplicity: "Eat food, not too much, mostly plants." Pollen's latest book, *Food Rules: An Eater's Manual*, elaborates a bit more. Basically he says if your grandmother didn't cook with it and your fourth grader can't pronounce it, don't eat it. This has been our philosophy at the ranch for seventy years now and we agree with him wholeheartedly.

If you need a little scientific proof, Dr. Walter Willett from Harvard has a huge cohort study called the Health Professional Follow-Up Study with 42,000 males, 122,000 older female nurses, and a new batch of younger participants. From this study that is now four decades long, he has extrapolated that we are designed to eat mostly a Mediterranean-type diet. Fruits, vegetables, whole grains, legumes, and heart-healthy oils form the basis of the diet with fish, dairy, eggs, and poultry used more moderately. Red meat, saturated fat, refined grains, and sugar should be indulged in rarely. Read Dr. Willett's wonderful book *Eat, Drink, and Be Healthy* for more on his diet recommendations. Another great read called *The Blue Zones* by Dan Buettner shows that the longest-lived populations around the globe (Sardinians, Okinawans, Costa Ricans in the Nicoya Valley, and the Seventh-Day Adventists in Loma Linda) eat a diet rich in plant-based foods and have extraordinarily high rates of healthy centenarians.

What is clear is that plant-based foods are not only loaded with fiber and nutrients, they are also chock-full of phytochemicals (also known as nutraceuticals and functional foods) that prevent and even reverse disease. And one last thing about eating lots of fruits and vegetables: They are rich in potassium and very alkalizing to the body. A study conducted at the Jean Mayer Human Nutrition Research Center on Aging at Tufts University found that in 384 senior men and women, an alkaline diet favored maintenance of lean muscle mass in the decade from sixty-five to seventy-five years of age. The expected loss of lean muscle is about four and a half to five pounds in that decade. The folks that ate the most fruits and veggies only lost just under a pound of muscle. That is significant.

So, how does all this relate to the nonvegetarian recipes in the Pot? Well, they all have plant-based foods in them (grains and beans and veggies, too). You can always supplement with a salad and/or some steamed vegetables on the side or have some fruit for dessert. And where the recipes call for white rice or white pasta, consider brown rice and other whole grains and pastas. At this point, I wonder what the fellow who submitted the Tangy, Sticky Sushi-Style Rice recipe and who says, "Anybody who eats long-grain rice is a Communist" will say of me? According to the *New York Times*, a recent Harvard study found that just replacing a third of a serving of white rice with brown each day could reduce one's risk of type 2 diabetes by 16 percent. A serving is half a cup of cooked rice, so a third of a serving means as little as 2⅔ tablespoons of cooked rice. That's not a whole lot for all the benefits.

Beans are rich in antioxidants, too. And the more colorful the bean, the better. They actually rival the much pricier berries and wine in antioxidant levels, so they are a good choice indeed for anyone on a budget. Beans also stabilize blood sugar and help prevent cancers. Mexicans eat a lot of beans—about thirty-five pounds per person per year. Compare this to an American who may eat five or six pounds per year. Mexicans have a significantly lower incidence of colorectal cancer than Americans.

Beans can help blood sugar stabilization and prevent cancers. In his article titled "Beans Against Cancer?," Ralph Moss, PhD, writes that when "USDA scientists analyzed the colored seed coats of twelve different types of beans they found that these legumes contained many of the same antioxidants (such as anthocyanins) that are also found in pricier berries and fruits, and also in wine." He continues that populations that eat the greatest amount of colorful beans have significantly lower cancer rates.

Grains, too, contain antioxidants that have been largely overlooked because they are in the bound form. But recent studies show that bacteria in the intestines actually release them. Corn came out tops in antioxidants when compared to other grains and fruits and veggies in studies conducted by Dr. Rui Hai Liu at Cornell. Since Rancho La Puerta is in Mexico, and corn has been a staple here along with beans and squash from time immemorial, we cheered the results of this study.

If you are trying to watch your waistline, here is a little caution about calories: Beans and grains are great foods, but calorically speaking, they are very condensed. One half cup (the size of a half of a baseball) of cooked beans or grains contains one hundred to one hundred and twenty-five calories. Contrast those calories with lettuce at nine calories per cup (a whole baseball full); most veggies have twenty-five to forty calories per cup and most fruits have between fifty and one hundred calories per cup. Also, some of the recipes herein contain quite a bit of butter and cream. You can always experiment with cutting these down. But remember it is the big picture that's important. If you eat a dish with lots of calories, just eat lots of nearly free veggies along with it. The key is balance and moderation.

Here at the ranch, where Roger is a frequent guest and presenter, we are big proponents of fresh, natural, local, seasonal, and organically grown foods. This, however, is an ideal that is easy for us to achieve with a year-round growing season and a large, beautiful organic garden. All that any of us can do as individuals is to do the best we can in a less than ideal world. We suggest that you look into community-supported agriculture in your area (also called subscription farming) (www.caff.org), community gardens (www.community-garden.org), edible school yards (www.edibleschoolyard.org), and farmers' markets (www.localharvest.org). If you want a book that teaches you to make better, healthier food choices from your local supermarket, read Dr. Marion Nestle's tome *What to Eat: An Aisle-by-Aisle Guide.* Because organics can be a bit pricey, download the Environmental Working Group's shopper's guide on the least sprayed conventionally grown fruits and veggies (www.food-news.org/walletguide.php).

Food *is* good medicine, especially when it is made with fresh, natural ingredients and cooked in a way to retain its nutrients, and especially when it is made with love. Because Roger is a film critic, let me recommend several good documentaries on the subject of food: A recently released DVD called *Food Matters* is important. Additionally, *Food, Inc.*, *The Future of Food*, *Fast Food Nation*, and *Dirt! The Movie* all speak volumes. If you want to educate yourself, reading is great, but in a time-compressed world, flicks are quicker. I know Roger would concur.

Enjoy cooking and eating the recipes herein. May your Pot always be filled with good things to eat.

Yvonne Nienstadt
Tecate, Baja California, Mexico
June 23, 2010 (Seventieth anniversary of Rancho La Puerta)

INTRODUCTION

by Anna Thomas

Dear Roger,

I know the first words of an introduction are supposed to be about how honored and flattered I am to be asked, et cetera and et cetera. And I am, all that and et cetera, too. But . . .

Are you kidding me?

All a kitchen needs is a rice cooker? There's nothing you can't cook in that Pot? You're putting this down on paper, between covers, for all time?

Offhand, I can think of about 1,000 things you couldn't cook in the Pot, starting with anything that requires a well-caramelized onion, which covers the first 500 or so, right on through the next 499 to Proust's madeleine.

But, Roger, you are generally the smartest guy in the room, full of sass and joie de vivre, and one of the most entertaining writers I know, so I begin to read. Within moments, I am going over Niagara Falls with you in that damned Pot.

Before the end of the first chapter, I understand. This is not so much a sales pitch for a kitchen appliance of arguable value, as it is an inspiring essay about food as personal history. Never mind the Pot. What I hear you saying is this: Cook! Cook to be useful, cook to take care of yourself, cook to be healthier, cook to feed the ones you love, cook to celebrate.

As for the Pot—of course, we all love the idea that somewhere out there is the Answer. When I had to camp out in a converted artist's studio with a tiny, temporary galley while my house was being remodeled—and six months stretched to three years—I decided the Answer was soup. I wrote a book about living the soup life and how those delicious and comforting soups answered so many questions. And I'll be damned if it didn't contain some of the same ideas I now find in your pages: come back to the fundamental, to what feels most important and rewarding about cooking. Use fresh food, cook, and have fun. Share with those you love.

So I keep reading—and I'm with you.

I'm with you through "the ancient mystery of the Orient" and "the Pot knows." You're a self-taught cook—me, too. And when you say, "This is just an idea, change anything and cook it your way," we are speaking with one voice. I always tell my readers, "It's my recipe on the page, but it's your soup in the pot." We are food-think twins!

And when you suggest that you could prepare many of the recipes in *The Vegetarian Epicure* in a rice cooker, I see that this is a health book, because what is healthier than a great, hearty LAUGH?!

I'm with you. I order a rice cooker. I promise to have nothing to do with words such as "neurofuzzy." When you say, "We don't want no stinking cookbooks," I know you mean it in the nicest way. And when I come to Aunt Mary—"Just throw in about enough, honey"—my heart is hers. I read her instructions about potatoes and I think, "Every book about food needs some poetry."

But when you say you can cook anything but a soufflé in your Pot—Roger, I must ask, can you caramelize an onion in it? You are "an American cook, Urbana born"—but I'm Polish. A wandering Pole, born in Stuttgart, weaned in Detroit, now a vegetarian in California—but wherever I am, I must have that well-caramelized onion!

Your Basic Soup Recipe? Not mine, buddy. Where is the caramelized onion? Where are the flavor-enriching techniques, such as tossing a few vegetables into a hot oven to roast until they are browned and glazed with their own sweet juices? Or quickly toasting spices in a skillet to free their true natures? Still, I try to be tolerant—until I read these words: "You can help your soup a little with bouillon cubes and instant stock mixes."

Bouillon cubes? Yikes! Roger!

Brooding on your words in the silent dark of night, though, I remember that I once did something like that myself. It was at Trail Camp, twelve thousand feet up Mount Whitney, the last place to pitch a tent before the hundred switchbacks and the thin air of the summit. That night I sprinkled a soup powder into a tiny titanium pot, over a camp stove the size of your hand. The few fresh vegetables I added were an unimaginable luxury. We had carried them up in our packs—and when you pack for that trip, you cut your toothbrush in half because it weighs too much. That was one of the most delicious soups of all time.

So, Reader, if you find yourself at a rocky campsite somewhere above twelve thousand feet on a freezing night . . . go ahead, use the instant stock mix. I give you permission.

But in those other instances—such as when you are at home, in a kitchen, near a refrigerator or a market—when you come to those words about the bouillon, do the right thing.

Stop and have a good laugh. Then proceed and make a fine soup or stew, using fresh ingredients. This is not a hard thing to do. For those of you who are not Aunt Mary, I have contributed to this book a few recipes adapted to the one-speed mulishness of the Pot. And if you are Aunt Mary, just make it work for you, honey!

And, Roger, my dear friend—though I groaned at references to canned soups and powders, in the end I decided to laugh. Because we really are telling folks the same thing: COOK!

Home cooking is slipping away from us. A generation of people watches celebrity chefs prepare food on TV shows—then orders out. This is not good. Where is Aunt Mary? So I will stop grousing about cans and caramelized onions, and will rejoice in the metamessage of your witty, tasty words: cook. You can do it, and you'll be glad you did. Even you, in your dorm room . . . You, in your studio . . . You, teenager, taxi driver, starving actor . . .

I salute you, Roger, for invoking the ancient spirit of the Pot. Your Pot is the rice cooker. Mine is the soup kettle. But the spirit is the same. The ancient and ever-new spirit of the generous Pot, the welcoming Pot, the steaming Pot around which friends and family can gather. The Pot that is part of your life.

Your friend in food and all,
Anna

1

I AM A
COMPETENT
COOK

I am a competent cook. Those at my table usually enjoy what I serve them. I am not, however, an educated or gourmet cook, and my methods are rough and ready. I've tried a few fancy recipes, but more for my own entertainment. There was a period in the early 1970s when I had broken up with a woman I did a lot of cooking with, and in loneliness I filled the long evenings by plundering cookbooks for recipes. Steamed trout. Chicken masala in a pastry-sealed pot. For weeks I recycled a Chinese red cooking liquid, constantly renewed, inflamed by stories of such liquids preserving a line of descent for a thousand years. This was during a period when I was doing a lot of drinking. In my experience, a woman who calls herself a gourmet cook may be a gourmet cook, but a man who calls himself a gourmet cook, unless he does it for a living, may be an alcoholic. There is nothing quite like sitting at the kitchen table, waiting for a pot to boil, sipping some wine, and paging ambitiously through *The New York Times Cookbook*. I still have the original Craig Claiborne version, not because the newer ones are not better, but because this one is stained and greasy and dog-eared, and has clippings stuffed into it. The splashes on the page for Country Captain are memorials to several confused but joyous evenings. On weekends I would mix myself a gin martini and keep it in the freezing compartment between sips. When I had broken the crust on the chicken masala and a thick cloud of curry mist escaped into the room, I would play "Also Sprach Zarathustra" on the *2001* sound track album at top volume on my hi-fi set. I recommend this music to accompany the presentation to the table of all main dishes, except oatmeal.

It was at that time I acquired *Quick and Easy Chinese Cooking*, by Kenneth H. C. Lo. Now there's a book with stains on almost every page. I got a cheap wok and a wooden spatula and took up stir-frying. I also used the steam tray to steam foods. This method quickly replaced most of my other methods, and although I stopped drinking in 1979, I never for a second stopped stir-frying. If I were for some reason alone at home, I rarely went to a restaurant by myself. After seeing *The Lonely Guy* with Steve Martin, that became too painful. It was not a great movie, but there was a shot in it showing a Lonely Guy sitting all by himself at a restaurant table that has haunted me. Why do you think so many solitary diners are so deeply involved in books? Because they are big readers?

I like to read while eating alone, because there is something in my mind that abhors a vacuum, and I cannot sit there and bless the universe for the beauty of the sprout. I won't watch TV during meals because my mother wouldn't let me. The radio is no good because I can't just sit there *listening*. I will read anything, but I prefer to be reading a long novel, for example, by Dickens or Trollope. Some guy could start reading some short novel and the damn thing could run out on him. How well I remember reading my first Stendhal later in life and discovering that he is *funny*, which no one ever told me.

All of which has nothing to do with the purpose of this little book. It is simply to establish that I enjoy cooking. I still do, even though I stopped drinking in 1979 and, for that matter, stopped eating in 2006. I cook for others, partly to make myself useful and mostly because I can have dinner on the table while most people are still spinning their wheels. As I have grown older, I have grown simpler and more a creature of habit. My wife, Chaz, tells me that everything I cook tastes the same and even looks about the same. This is not unfair. I like green, red, and yellow peppers, green vegetables, onions, corn, carrots, and tomatoes, combined with other elements and various creatures from the land, the sea, and the sky. Often I like to season them with hot dried or fresh peppers or various bottled Indian or Caribbean sauces or Worcestershire. I am of the school that says a little Splenda never killed anybody.

So you see what you're dealing with here. Every suggestion in this book comes with the same injunction: *This is just an idea. Change anything or everything in the recipe, and cook it your way.* That is the way I use all cookbooks, and that is the way you should use mine. When I got my first Mac in the late 1980s, my guru, Don Crabb, told me: "They make every software program follow the same basic commands. If you know the commands, you know how to do everything." It is the same with a wok. And for the noble Pot.

2

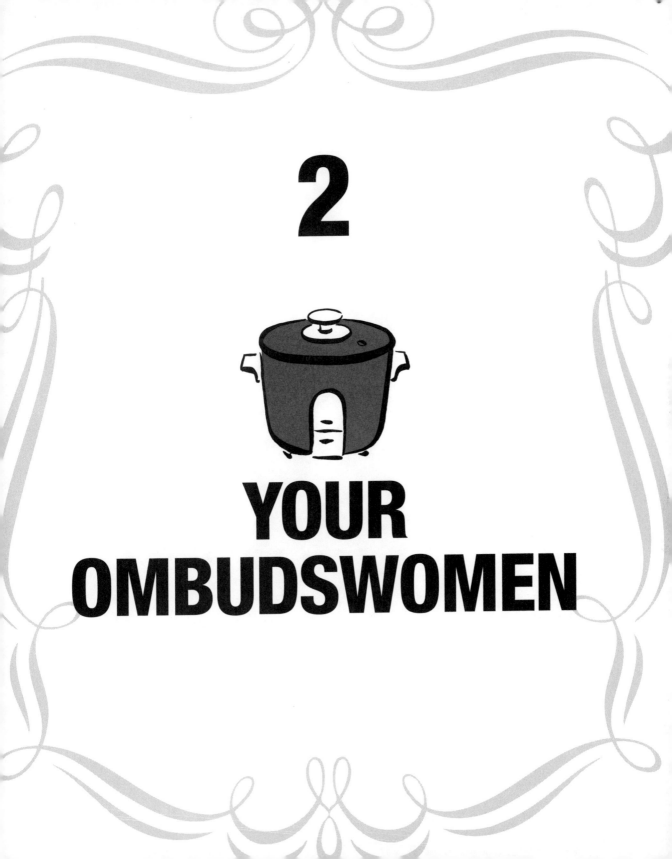

YOUR OMBUDSWOMEN

I have enlisted in this enterprise two innocent bystanders. They do not endorse this book. They have been recruited simply to protect you. When I say they are friends of mine, the fact that they have agreed to this is proof. One is Anna Thomas, the celebrated author of the international best-sellers *The Vegetarian Epicure; The Vegetarian Epicure: Book Two; The New Vegetarian Epicure*; and *Love Soup*. The other is Yvonne Nienstadt, author of *Cal-a-Vie's Gourmet Spa Cookery: Recipes for Health and Wellness* and nutrition director of Rancho La Puerta Fitness Resort and Spa in Tecate, Mexico.

I met Anna Thomas in 1976, when she and her then-husband, Gregory Nava, brought their film *The Confessions of Amans* to the Chicago International Film Festival. It was the story of a medieval Spanish monk who walked to the Middle East and learned the principles of mathematics and a great deal about life. I considered it brilliant. They shared an Academy Award nomination for their screenplay for the great *El Norte* (1983), which Anna produced and Gregory directed. They collaborated again on *A Time of Destiny* (1988) and *Mi Familia* (1995), and they wrote *Frida* (2002).

Although it is against my principles to become personal friends with filmmakers, I liked them so quickly and sincerely that I found that rule impossible to enforce. You would, too. I spent many happy evenings in their Los Angeles home (where the Independent Feature Project was founded in the living room) and later in their hilltop Running Ridge Ranch in Ojai, where in her kitchen I had many meals, including her mushroom soup made with wild mushrooms collected by Gregory, once the head of the local mushroom fanciers' society.

Her first cookbook was one of the most influential cookbooks in the history of modern vegetarian cuisine. She had been cooking for friends in film school at UCLA, and noticed she was eating less and less meat, and finally none. She devised her recipes from fresh seasonal ingredients, testing things and making them up. That should be your inspiration. She sent her manuscript to Alfred A. Knopf, the august New York publishers of such giants as James Beard and Julia Child, and they bought it instantly. "They were a little amazed to discover it had been written by a kid," she told me. We had dinner once at Charlie Trotter's, the finest restaurant in Chicago. She saw kohlrabi broth on the menu and mused, "Just the other day, my son Teddy asked me, 'Mom, how about some of that kohlrabi broth!'"

Charlie invited us back to his kitchen and proudly presented his copies of her first two cookbooks, which were battered, dog-eared, and splashed with things. "I own thousands of cookbooks," Trotter told her. "These are the only two I can say I have cooked every single recipe from." In my opinion, you could prepare many of them in a rice cooker. Of course, in my opinion, you can prepare almost anything in a rice cooker, including a recipe I am working on now, So-Called Pot Roast.

In asking Anna to write her introduction, I suggested she say something like: "Roger, Roger, Roger. You know I love you, and a rice pot is fine, but for recipes, your poor readers would be better off reading another cookbook—mine, for example."

Every time I see Yvonne Nienstadt, I tell her she is the most brilliant woman I have ever met. I tell her this even in the presence of Chaz, who smiles benignly. She knows how I am. There is nothing she doesn't know about nutrition, and she is not one of these twig-eating ascetics who walk around looking worried all day. She has a big, hearty laugh, and she loves food, and she merely hopes you don't kill yourself with what you're eating, which is hard to argue with. After surgery deprived me of the ability to eat in the manner to which I had become accustomed, I had to switch to a liquid diet that came in cans. I know someone who has lived on the canned stuff for thirty years. We nevertheless hurried back to Rancho as soon as we could, because although their food is terrific, it is also the most peaceful, spacious, beautiful, and enriching place I have ever been, and not the most expensive.

As is my habit, I always turn up for Yvonne's afternoon lecture on diet and nutrition. It is not one of those horrible lectures at other spas in which clichés are recycled out of half-remembered Weight Watchers classes. Yvonne stays on top of the latest research, keeps an open mind, thinks vegetarian eating is good for you but doesn't insist on it, brings you to your senses about salt and fat, and knows all about vitamins and minerals, by which she doesn't mean bring home lots of bottles from the health store. She speaks fluently and clearly, with every fact at her command, and answers your questions. She doesn't get all wound up. In fact, once I walked into a meditation workshop and who was sitting cross-legged on the rug but Yvonne. Even then she doesn't say you'll find nirvana. She only says you might be able to dial down and clear your mind a little.

Yvonne's lectures always put me right to sleep. That is because I always get up in time for the Rolling Hills Hike or the Garden Breakfast Hike, and when she speaks after lunch, I get . . . uh . . . my eyelids . . . uh. . . . Yvonne knows this weakness and is fond of me despite it. "After all these times, at one time or another, you have been wide awake during every portion of my remarks," she assured me. "I know you're not dozing because you're not interested."

When I broke the news to her that my eating days were over, she looked interested, not horrified. A few days after returning home, I received an e-mail from her titled "Dead Food!" She wrote: "Now eating out of a can has kept you alive, but eating fresh and vital foods will help you to heal.

Besides, you are a special person and need premium fuel! Freshly made vegetable juices mixed with the canned formula would be an improvement. . . ." Then she sent me some info about homemade G-tube formulas, but I won't go into that because I am not your doctor.

Rancho has its own organic farm, and in some seasons 80 percent of what you eat is grown right there. This is no sacrifice, because I'm not kidding when I say it's delicious. Yvonne supervises the nutrition and works with the chef on his recipes. In deciding to write *The Pot*, I asked her if she would look it over and point out anything that struck her as being unhealthy, unwise, or lethal. This she has agreed to do as a life-saving measure. She thinks a rice cooker is more useful, but does *not* endorse any of the recipes, and possibly would refuse to eat some of them—except with her revisions and substitutions, which is how you should regard them, too. This is not an instruction book. It is an evocation of the ancient spirit of the Pot.

3

YOUR
BOOK

This is a little book for people who would like to be able to prepare meals simply and quickly in a very limited amount of space—not even necessarily in a kitchen. I am thinking of you, student in your dorm room. You, solitary writer, artist, musician, potter, plumber, builder, hermit. You, with a corner of your desk or table free. You, parents on tight schedules with kids. You, who are beginning to believe you should pay more attention to breakfast. You, night watchman. You, obsessed computer programmer or weary Web-worker. You, lovers who like to cook together but don't want to put anything in the oven. You, in the witness protection program. You, nutritional wingnut. You, in a wheelchair. And you, serving in uniform. You, person on a small budget who wants healthy food. You, shut-in. You, recovering campaign worker. You, movie critic at Sundance. You, factory worker sick of frozen meals. You, people in Werner Herzog's documentary about life at the South Pole. You, early riser skipping breakfast. You, teenager home alone. You, rabbi, pastor, priest, monk, nun, waitress, community organizer, nurse, starving actor, taxi driver, long-haul driver. Yes, even you.

4

GET
THE POT

First, get the Pot. You need the simplest rice cooker made. It comes with two speeds: Cook and Warm. Sometimes Warm is named Hold. Not expensive. Now you're all set to cook meals for the rest of your life on two square feet of counter space, including an area to do a little slicing and dicing. No, I am not putting you on the Rice Diet. Eat what you like. You can get fat with a rice cooker, or you can get thin. Your choice. Depends on what you put in the Pot.

It is a squat cooking utensil that some find unlovely. When I regard one, I remember many happy meals it has given me. "Form follows function," as Louis Sullivan instructs us, and the Pot is a beautiful expression of that idea. It is as pure and uncomplicated as possible—a pot with a lid, a handle, and one control that clicks between Warm and Hold.

How does this Pot work? We will begin with a conundrum. You put Minute Rice and the correct amount of water into the Pot, and click to Cook. Minutes later, the Pot clicks over to Warm. The rice waits inside, cooked perfectly. Tomorrow night, you put in whole grain organic rice and the correct amount of water into the Pot, and click to Cook. Forty-five minutes or an hour later, the Pot clicks over to Warm. Again, the rice is perfectly cooked.

How does the Pot know which kind of rice you put into it? It has no dials or settings. As far as you can tell, there is only an electric heating element beneath. It doesn't look to you like there's room for anything else to hide. How does the Pot know how long to cook the rice? It is an ancient mystery of the Orient. Don't ask questions you don't need the answers to. The point here is to save you some time and money. If you want gourmet cooking, you aren't going to learn about it here. The Pot knows. The eternal dilemma: Which rice? Minute Rice cooks fine in the Pot, if you will but follow the exact instructions on the box. Later, I will instruct you not to read instructions. That's further down. For now, read the Minute Rice box! It is called Minute Rice for a reason. If you let it cook for half an hour, you are going to be poking around in your Pot looking for your rice. Minute Rice is for when you're in a big hurry and nutrition be damned. Minute Rice has been painstakingly deprived of its vitamins, which are fed to boars and captive chickens. If you have time, always use real rice. Brown rice is good for you. Buy it in large sizes at the grocery store—any store, not just Whole Foods.

It can be very inexpensive. Through Amazon, you can purchase fifty pounds of premium-quality brown rice. I hate to think how long that would last you. I recommend a smaller size. Ten pounds short-grain, $17.85. Twenty-five pounds aromatic long-grain, $38.90. Shop around. Check the bulk stores. Start with a pound, and see how long that lasts you. A pound might be the best idea for you.

It doesn't have to be rice. Don't overlook other grains and pastas. All grains cook fine in the Pot, even hominy, if you will but follow the exact instructions they come with. Experiment. Basmati rice is nice. (Note: Someone wrote in saying "Oh, no! I can't eat this or that kind of rice! I'm allergic!" Then don't eat it. Do you think I want to give you the hives?)

5

TO REPEAT, GET THE POT

I am not a French gourmet. I am a practical cook. An American, Urbana-born, and go at things as I have taught myself, freestyle, and will make a cookbook in my own way. When I cook, I want to eat in the immediate future. I can cook for my wife or the whole family as easily as for me. And, as Travis Bickle says, "Anytime, anywhere." To be sure, health problems have prevented me from eating. That did not discourage my cooking. It became an exercise more pure, freed of biological compulsion. You will not see me on TV in the middle of the night, hawking rice cookers. This book is strictly pro bono.

To repeat, get the Pot. I may have to do a certain amount of repeating, to emphasize how simple this whole business is. I've had about a dozen Pots over the years. I always buy Zojirushi. I have no idea if they are the best. I use a three-cup and a ten-cup. There is even a twenty-cup Zojirushi, if you are the Soup Nazi. We are still using the three-cup

Zojirushi our assistant, Carol Iwata, gave us as a wedding present eighteen years ago. It has gone to the Sundance Film Festival with me. This is the bottom line: Get the Pot.

There are many models and sizes. Have nothing to do with anything "Micom Programmable." Nothing to do with words like "Neuro Fuzzy." No dials or "settings." Nothing fancy. You will only cost yourself money and mess things up. If a rice cooker comes with more than two pages of instructions, you've overspent. I am saving us money. What you want is your basic Pot with two speeds: Cook and Warm. Sometimes it says Hold instead of Warm. Maybe it will say it in Japanese. You'll figure it out.

There are countless rice cooker cookbooks. We don't want no stinking cookbooks. Think of your Pot as being like a Macintosh: Once you figure out how the thing works, you don't need a manual.

Whatever your gender, you will do this like a man, by refusing to read the instructions. Or a woman like my aunt Mary, who copied down and traded recipes for a lifetime, and never used a single one of them. When she was in the kitchen, she was on automatic. She had two speeds: Cook and Serve. She did not know how to measure salt. "Just throw in about enough, honey," she told me. This was her poetic wisdom about how to estimate the number of potatoes sufficient for a meal:

One potato
For every member of the family.
One potato for the pot.
And one last tater, honey,
For fear of later company.

We are her kind of cook. We try. We learn. We experiment. When we have absorbed the principle of the Pot, we will find ourselves daydreaming about new combinations. Can you cook potatoes in the Pot? Of course you can, and boiled eggs, too. You can cook about everything but a soufflé.

6

BREAKFAST FOR YOUR LIFETIME

If you eat nothing else for breakfast, eat oatmeal. This simple food tastes very good. Prepared properly, it has a pleasing texture on the tongue. I prefer it slightly al dente. Oatmeal is high in fiber, decreasing your anxiety before a dreaded colonoscopy. The FDA says it can lower cholesterol and reduce the risk of heart disease. It attacks bad cholesterol but not good cholesterol. It lowers blood glucose levels. It is loaded with B vitamins. It can help you lose weight. You don't get hungry before lunch. It contains hardly any fat. If you take it with milk or soy milk, it adds protein and calcium.

I like stone-ground organic oatmeal. Put in the Pot as much as you need, and the specified amount of water. The water is important. I like my oatmeal al dente, but if you like yours a little softer, with experience you can make small adjustments in the amount of water. There is no perfect ratio. As Aunt Mary would say, "Honey, be sure to use the right amount."

Now we are going to work on that oatmeal. Of course, you can simply *eat* it, but even if you're in a hurry, you can combine it with other ingredients to improve its taste and nutrition.

Look for some unground flaxseed. Never mind why "unground." It's good for you. Believe me, there's an excellent reason why you don't want to grind your flaxseed and let it sit around. I'm cooking here, and I don't have time to go into endless details.

Grind it fresh in a mortar and pestle. You don't have a mortar and pestle? People these days want everything done for them. Do like the Indians did and grind it with the end of a stick in the depression of a boulder. Measure out a generous teaspoon for every serving. If for some reason you have one of those little grinders for fresh coffee beans, you can use it for your flaxseed. Clean carefully. Your company may not notice a little coffee in your oatmeal, but flaxseed in your coffee is frowned upon.

Speaking of coffee, for years I had a foolproof method of making instant coffee taste like the real thing, rich and full-bodied. What I would do is add a little instant Postum to the boiling water. Few calories, no fat or salt, good for you. Incredibly, *they stopped making Postum in 2007*! I guess it broke the law by not containing corn syrup. Now eight-ounce jars are going for $30 on eBay. No, Postum was not what Li'l Orphan Annie drank.

Now you have your oatmeal. You can substitute any grain of your choice. Even amaranth, seen as the favorite side dish in *The Mummy: Tomb of the Dragon Emperor*. On top of my oatmeal, I like to use low-fat Silk soy milk. Use regular milk, rice milk—whatever you like.

Have a small or medium chopping board and a nice knife. Slice the fruit of your choice into smallish pieces. Any fruit except something like watermelon. I shouldn't have to be telling you this. Slice your bananas, your peaches, your apples, pears, plums, apricots, strawberries, your kiwi. Throw in your blueberries, your blackberries, your boysenberries, your this berry, your that berry. Drop in maybe a couple of dried prunes or some raisins. No, hotshot. Not all the fruits at once. We're making breakfast, not fruit compote. Let's say two fruits together are nice. Bananas and peaches

make Peaches 'n' Cream. Mmmm! Chaz loves 'em.

While you're doing this, your oatmeal is already cooking. Figure out the hard way when to add the fruit to the Pot so it tastes best and doesn't get all boiled to death on you. Okay. Fruit's in. Slam the lid back down. Cook and Warm. The Pot watches itself. It will wait there for you a long time. Find out the hard way what's too long. If the result looks like a potato pancake, that was too long. On the other hand, you can make a sort of half-assed potato pancake, although not crisp on the bottom, that way. You can even start with instant potatoes, if you're a fool. Chop in some onions on the far turn. Throw in onions, peppers, and mushrooms, and when they're thundering down the home stretch, some stirred-up eggs, and you have what down home we call Skillet. You can fine-tune how mushy you want it—not very, I'd say.

Back to oatmeal. Take a good look at the label on that microwave oatmeal you've been eating. It's probably loaded with salt, corn syrup, and palm and coconut oils— the two deadliest oils on the planet. It's a dangerous travesty of the healthy food it pretends to be. But it's high fiber, you say? Terrific. You can die of a heart attack during a perfect bowel movement.

7

YOUR
SOUPS

Now you have mastered the Pot. Every recipe works the same way. By trial and error, you learn to adjust the amount of water, for example, to steam spinach versus steaming broccoli. Most Pots come with a circular insert that holds veggies or eggs a little off the bottom, for optimum steaming. Or use a little dish or cup. If you can steam it, you can steam it in the Pot. Be vigilant. Too much water will steam it limp. Too little, it could boil dry. The Pot knows when rice is perfectly cooked, but it can get too carried away sometimes with other ingredients. You will learn how to monitor the Pot when you're making something like soup, which you don't want to cook all the way down.

Let's make some soup. Assemble your ingredients. Throw them in the Pot. Add enough water to make it soup. That is your Basic Soup Recipe. Of course, a nice soup stock is better than water. If you are in a dorm room or a monk's cell, you may not have any soup stock handy. You can help your soup a little with various bouillon cubes and instant stock mixes. Just don't fool yourself that they are real soup stocks. We will discuss a Secret Soup Weapon in the next chapter.

I have been known to start out with a can of Health Valley or Pritikin soup, usually not one of those high-sodium big-time soups, and then add fresh ingredients. I have also been known to start with Health Valley vegetarian chili and add ground beef, spices, and chopped onion late in the day. You will probably want a small onion. I use a larger one. Sometimes so large, you would be shocked.

When you have everything in, slam down the lid. This watched Pot boils. Click to Warm when the soup seems to be getting about right. If it looks undercooked, add a little more water and keep going.

You will also learn to add the ingredients in the reverse order of how long you think they'll take to cook. For example, dried beans first. Even let them sit in water and Warm for a while, to soften them up. If you're in a hurry, throw them in and boil them. Dried beans can take it. Never put in meat and chicken so soon it will overcook. There are no rules. You are Aunt Mary. "Put it in at the right time, honey."

Of course, you prefer fresh vegetables, organic when possible, and if you could, you would only patronize the farmers' market. But sometimes you have to make do. If you have a freezing compartment handy, keep a selection of frozen veggies on hand. Peas, corn, chopped carrots, chopped cabbage, green beans, okra, baby sprouts, broccoli, chopped spinach or collard greens, "mixed vegetables," "succotash," mushrooms packed in water—whatever.

You probably skimmed right over the words *baby sprouts*. I don't understand why so many people don't like brussels sprouts. The noble sprout ranks with broccoli and cabbage as the most nutritious of all vegetables. It is also delicious. I love 'em. I like the little al dente feel you get if they haven't been cooked to mush. If you start with fresh sprouts, remove any damaged outer leaves and cut a cross in the stem to hasten cooking. If you're really in a hurry, cut them in half. For soup, cut them to a size so they're not ostentatious. You don't want to dip your spoon in your soup and come up with a big old sprout. If you think you don't like how they taste, don't eat them unadorned

and unaccompanied. Lose them in a soup or stew. Good for you.

Anyway, the basic principle is: Rarely be satisfied with just opening a can of soup. Your body needs its veggies. Get them in there somehow. Fresh, dried, frozen, any way is better for you than no veggies. If you start with canned soup, consider that your base or stock. The photo on the label looks good, but the ingredients have been waiting a long time and need some reinforcements.

Now I am going to suggest something that may sound, I dunno, naive or simplistic. There is no better last-second addition to a soup than frozen peas. I stir them into hot soup and *immediately* serve the soup. The frozen peas thaw out on the way to the table. They look delightfully green, taste crunchy and fresh, and add to the general interest. I am sure this sounds barbaric, but I have been known to enjoy a can of tomato soup with just some frozen peas added at the last moment.

When I mention "sodium," be aware that most canned soups are overloaded with it. Some single cans contain more than half a day's ideal amount. They're lethal. "Low salt" mainline brands are still too high. You're better off with Health Valley and Pritikin. Read the label. People who have a can of soup thinking they're doing something virtuous will pay the price with high blood pressure and increased risk of stroke.

8

YOUR SECRET
SOUP WEAPON

When you see coverage of the Sundance Film Festival on channels like E!, you get the idea it consists mainly of celebrities sitting on decks in the sunshine, wearing their ski fashion wear and mirrored sunglasses, with snow-covered slopes behind them. At night, they hang out at parties with music so loud they have to shout at the twits who are interviewing them. They like to do this. They all look so much the same you can barely remember which one just survived heartbreak on the cover of the *National Enquirer*. When you see a real actor like Tilda Swinton at Sundance, it's because she's there to see the movies.

Parties have nothing to do with Sundance. The festival is a relentless morning-to-midnight schedule of movies, most of them pretty good, many of them in conflict with each other. A movie critic who goes to a party or a group free-feed is missing a movie, maybe two. It's just that simple. The biggest films play at 7:00 and 9:30 P.M. every night at the big Eccles Center. How can you see those and be at a party? How late can you stay up and still make the 9:00 A.M. screening at the Library?

On the other hand, how can you sustain life on muffins, chocolate chip cookies, and candy sold in the lobbies? You can't. That's why you see the genuine true-blue Sundancers at Albertson's supermarket the night before the festival opens, stocking up on stuff to see them through. Although a great many attendees stay in rented condos (sometimes so many in the same one the landlord has no idea), they are not in the mood to whip up three-course meals in their kitchenette area. After we got our Pot, I decided to take it to Sundance. The three-cup size fit nicely in my carry-on.

At Albertson's that night I was strolling down the aisles in my Supermarket Reverie Mode when my eyes fell on Bear Creek Soup Mix. There was an array of dried soup mixes with the usual enticing photographs on the labels. I like potato soup, always have, and so I bought the Creamy Potato Mix. Zero fat—all the Bear Creek mixes are fat-free. It wasn't that low in sodium, however. One cup contains 900 mg, or 37 percent of your recommended value. Soup makers seem intent on driving up Americans' blood pressure. To avoid that, you need a truly salt-free soup.

But I didn't have a cup of Bear Creek. That's where the Secret Weapon element comes into play. I started with more like a quarter cup, added water and my other ingredients, and the soup was up to speed. As a soup, their Creamy Potato is delicious. As a base, it is magical, transforming your more mundane ingredients into a tasty blend. It comes in envelopes with eight- and sixteen-cup servings, so you seal up the unused mix for next time. They make everything from broccoli to chili. But, alas, there is a catch. . . .

9

YOUR SODIUM LEVEL

The only problem with Bear Creek was that troublesome sodium level. If you're not worried, I doubt you can find a better-tasting dry soup mix. But I was worried. Yvonne Nienstadt, our Rancho La Puerta nutrition expert, told me that in the case of most people's high blood pressure, salt is by far the most important determining factor. I'd heard the same thing from the nutrition researcher and lecturer Dr. Jay Kenney at the Pritikin Longevity Center, who compared horrifying statistics showing that Pima Indians in Mexico have heart attack and stroke rates at extremely low levels, while Pima Indians in America, who are genetically identical, are dropping like flies. Well, Jay didn't mention flies. The reason: their diet. "Eat the corn, not the corn chip," Jay told us sternly.

If you're thinking only about the problem of blood pressure, you can essentially forget about lowering your blood pressure with meditation and stress reduction. Oh, things like that are fine (did I mention Yvonne is a yoga practitioner?), but when it comes to blood pressure, there is one thing you need to focus on, and that is sodium—period. A lot of people have heart trouble, minor strokes, or bypass surgery and are advised by their doctors to "cut back" on their salt. Their idea of "cutting back" is vague at best—and, for that matter, they have no idea of where the sodium is in their diet. So what if they don't salt soup that already comes with 1,000 mg in a cup?

There are countless brands of instant soups, and I went looking for the perfect one. Almost all of them contained way too much salt. I did, however, find one brand with *zero* salt and *zero* fat. What is the name? Bean Cuisine. They make ten varieties, mostly bean-based, although they make an exception for Sante Fe Corn Chowder. Wouldn't you know that one has 10 mg of sodium per cup? A little salt won't kill you. If you had 160 cups of it a day, you'd be asking for trouble.

You're wondering, how exciting can bean soup taste? Just from scratch, their bean soups don't taste bad at all, especially after your taste buds have leveled out after years of being salt-cured daily. And the lowly bean is one of nature's nearly perfect foods, containing even protein. Its fiber content is good for you. You're still asking, how does it taste?

I'm going to get around that question by asking another one: What do you put in it? The Pot has nearly unlimited versatility in what it can prepare for you, and is so quick and easy to use it's a cinch to doctor your meal with a breathtaking variety of ingredients. Consider any dry soup mix as a starter. Add protein, spices, and sauces to it. Play around with recipes. Try stuff out. Every

recipe is only a suggestion. Most of the time I don't use one at all, and simply combine whatever I have on hand or find in the house. Try to think of the Pot as a recipe-neutral utensil. When somebody gives you a skillet, do you ask if it comes with a cookbook? No. Form follows function. When woks made their big splash in America, people were fighting to buy wok cookbooks. What you need is to master the *principle* of the wok.

With beans, as I suggested above, let them soak to soften. Overnight, if you have the time. In the Pot on Warm, if you want to hasten the process. Or just start them boiling. The hell with them. The crucial question is, what goes in the Pot after (or instead of) your beans?

10

YOUR
PROTEINS

Well, any meat, obviously. Beef, chicken, pork, goat, wild boar, minotaur, hot dogs, hamburger. Cut into bite-sized pieces. Fish, you have to be careful not to overcook. Canned tuna and salmon are useful. Easy on the tuna to save the dolphins. Use chilled shrimp, but don't let it cook until it gets too tough. Add fresh shrimp toward the end. Delicate fish, wait to read my salmon recipe.

No rare meat is going to emerge from the Pot. Stage your ingredients on your rough estimate of cooking time. Long-cooking grains first. Longer-cooking vegetables, like carrots and small or diced potatoes, before veggies like snow peas. Onions depending on how you like them.

Using the staging method, you can make stews. The trick is to adjust the amount of water. Be sure any grains, meats, and longer-cooking vegetables are mostly cooked with the water they need, then add quicker vegetables, but limit the amount of water. Monitor. This is a skill you develop with experience. You might want to augment the flavor with canned bouillon, instant soup, or canned diced tomatoes. Or begin with a can of stew and throw in veggies. Canned stews are mostly loaded with salt, which you will cut with the veggies, but remember that any sodium you add to the Pot, you add to yourself. If you are using a larger size Pot, the sodium in a can of soup or stew can be diluted further. Don't forget Brunswick stew.

Especially when a grocery store is not available, try the various vegetable proteins, including seitan. Tofu should be refrigerated, but it travels well. Cut up tofu into bite-sized pieces. Also try textured soy protein, which comes pretending to be beef chunks, chicken chunks, or hamburger. It is dry and can be taken anywhere. Soak in cold water before cooking. Properly cooked, it's fine. And healthy.

11

YOUR HERBS
AND SPICES

I mentioned the life-extending benefits of a low-salt, low-fat diet. This is up to you. Throw in salt by the handful if you want to. I don't care. Aunt Mary would get nervous: "Don't you think that's about enough?" Always use oils very sparingly. Even my pals at Pritikin say you can use a little olive oil. That means a *little*, Chef Boyardee.

Every cookbook I've ever opened encouraged you to experiment with lots of different herbs and spices. I suspect a lot of people have shelves lined with little spice bottles they never open, and stick to a few favorite spices. All I can add to this is, be especially quick to use fresh herbs like basil. If you have dried ones, rub them between your palms before throwing them into the Pot.

I happen to have a weakness for spicy foods, but not spicy to a ridiculous degree. I know there are people who subscribe to magazines about hot peppers that carry things to a bizarre extreme, and I knew a guy once who was in pain for thirty-six hours because he didn't believe the label on something called Burn Yo Ass Hot Sauce: "Removes the spots on your driveway!" You're not trying to prove anything.

I believe curry powders have an incredibly appetizing aroma.

12

YOUR
SAUCES

A gourmet cook would never stoop to adding bottled sauces to menus, but I stoop all the time. There are three I am especially fond of.

The Original Lea & Perrins Worcestershire Sauce. No oil. Very low salt. You know how Lea and Perrins invented it? They owned the chemist shop in Worcestershire. A colonel in the British army came home from serving the Raj, and told them about a great sauce he had tasted in India. John Wheeley Lea and William Henry Perrins worked together with great care to assemble the correct ingredients. They left them to ferment in a barrel down in the cellar. The colonel never came home again from India. Three years later, Lea & Perrins remembered the barrel, but they couldn't remember what they put into it. So, they invented Worcestershire sauce. It is still made in the original factory on Midlands Road. The neighborhood smells like Bloody Marys.

Marie Sharp's Exotic Sauce. Made in

Belize, the former British Honduras. You were thinking of Grenada. Cooked up first in the kitchen by Marie and her family, now by twenty employees who are like family. No salt. No oil. A little spicy and very delicious. Ingredients: fresh green mangoes, tamarind, raisins, ginger, sugar, vinegar, onions, garlic, habanero peppers, and spices. Sold in stores and on the Web. Marie makes a lot of hot sauces, but the Exotic Sauce does not alarmingly claim to remove spots from your driveway.

Worcestershire and Marie Sharp's Exotic are the two best steak sauces in the world. Sometimes I get to the point where I add a little Worcestershire, Marie Sharp's, or Saigon Sizzle to everything. Then I remember that nothing whets the appetite like the smell of curry cooking. However, there is, strictly speaking, no such thing as "curry powder." You can purchase the constituent ingredients and combine according to taste. Speaking of steak sauces, you will have noticed I do not recommend cooking steaks in the Pot. That would be a bad idea.

House of Tsang Saigon Sizzle Sauce. Contains some salt and oil. Use it when you go crazy mad. I do, several times a week. A nice addition to a stir-fry. How do you stir-fry in the Pot? You don't. Combine the ingredients of your stir-fry and put them in the Pot. Much lower oil that way. Start with rice or the grain of your choice, let it cook awhile, then throw in whatever you want in your stir-fry. Animal or vegetable protein, onions, peppers, mushrooms, bamboo shoots, baby corn, anything. Also try sweet and sour sauce (and throw in some pineapple chunks) or peanut sauce (and throw in some soy nuts). A few drops of sesame oil add aroma. I like to stir in some frozen peas at the last moment and let them cook on the way to the table.

Most stir-fries use onions. Onions need to be browned, not steamed, for such recipes. Pay great attention while doing so. Spray some Pam Olive Oil or a little oil on the bottom of the Pot, add chopped onions but no water, turn to Cook *very briefly,* and then add other ingredients.

There are countless other sauces. These are mine. There are countless combinations of grains and foods. You will be full, healthy, and happy. You will become the center of attention when you claim you can cook almost anything in the Pot. Take it from me. I put it in my Who's Who entry, and it has added immeasurably to my aura of mystery and intrigue.

13

YOUR
COMMENTS

■ **By sdr on November 1, 2008 6:36 P.M.**

Finally . . . a post for the stay-at-home housewife with not-so-much time on her hands (we're your target demographic, I know).

But will it rival my beloved Crock-Pot? That's what I really want to know. But I'm a sucker for a gadget, so the Amazon order is in and I'm determined to find out.

EBERT: You can try leaving it on Warm for an extended period, but keep an eye on it and unplug it if it causes any concern. I think you're safer with your beloved Crock-Pot. You probably have more than two square feet of counter space. Think what a treasure the Pot is for Asians who don't have kitchens as big as an indoor skating rink.

■ **By Brendan Frost on November 1, 2008 7:20 P.M.**

My God, this is a priceless entry for someone who fits TWO of your categories, college student and solitary writer. All the better because you posted this just as I was beginning to panic about my current extreme need to save money feeding myself. And what's more, you threw in witticisms and references, right down to Saul Bellow! For real, this post was crucial, thank you.

■ **By Kirsten on November 1, 2008 8:08 P.M.**

I love my cheap, $12.99 rice cooker. My eldest daughter has celiac disease and cannot eat traditional pastas and breads, so we live by our rice cooker and bread maker. We eat rice four days a week and I would die without it. Cut up some pork strips, add some gluten-free cream of mushroom soup, put it on top of the rice, add some green beans and a spinach salad with carrots and cucumber, a drizzle of Italian dressing (also gluten-free)—voilà—dinner for four for less than $20.

BTW, you'd be surprised how much of our food uses gluten as a binding agent. Half the stuff we used to eat is no longer allowed in my house.

■ By Jerry Roberts on November 1, 2008 8:43 P.M.

My wife and I got married two years ago and out of the few wedding gifts that were NOT towels, we ended up with a rice cooker. It was a Black and Decker sixteen-cup rice cooker (model RC426). We followed the instructions and the thing just ended up making a mess. It spewed water all over the place and there was so much steam that it made the cabinets wet. Was I doing something wrong? Or is this like microwave popcorn where you really can't trust the instructions?

We haven't used it since. It's been sitting in the corner of our dining room amid the stuff we will donate to Goodwill while I agonize over the decision to give it to the poor and have them inherit the same problem I had.

Our old manner of cooking rice was in a metal pot that we use on the stove. It doesn't gauge itself but it sure makes less of a mess.

EBERT: Shouldn't be one drop of spew. You were pranked by your friend. Never read the instructions. This blog entry is all you need. The instructions even tell you: "CAUTION! Do not cook anything but rice in this cooker!" Yeah, like the Pot gives a damn. The bastards are just trying to sell you some other pot.

■ By Robert of Taoyuan City, Taiwan, on November 1, 2008 9:34 P.M.

Dear Jerry Roberts, you wrote:
It spewed water all over the place and there was so much steam that it made the cabinets wet.

It spewed water all over the place? Sounds like you've put too much water into the rice (although, I have to say that it does that sometimes, even under normal circumstances). Also, did you wash the rice first until clear (about three times)? As a personal rule, the volume of rice you put into the cooker is also the volume of water, and a bit more, you use to cook it in. Or, be sure to only use the measuring cup that came with your cooking gadget. And yes, it's supposed to steam and wet the cabinets. I put mine under the kitchen exhaust fan.

■ By Somniferous on November 1, 2008 9:41 P.M.

Regarding your conundrum:
Minute Rice is a brand of parboiled rice.

It takes less time to cook because it has already been boiled in the husk. I have never cooked whole grain organic rice, but I believe it hasn't been parboiled. Because Minute Rice has already been boiled in the husk, it takes less time for the rice to become saturated; I imagine that this is not the case with whole grain organic rice. Once the rice is saturated and the residual water has boiled away, the temperature of the rice exceeds the boiling point, thus tripping the thermostat in the rice cooker—the rice cooker then switches to "Warming." Since it takes less time for the Minute Rice to become saturated, it achieves the "Warming" state faster than the whole grain organic rice. Of course, that's just one theory. Personally, I'm a fan of the Intelligent Pot.

■ By Nic Hautamaki on November 1, 2008 9:53 P.M.

As an expat living in China I can vouch for the awesomeness and surprising versatility that is the rice cooker. And yes, it most certainly is a critical device in the average small kitchen here.

■ By anjeee on November 1, 2008 11:08 P.M.

I can't believe you love House of Tsang sauce as much as I do! I have never found anyone else who used the sauce other than those I've turned on to it. I absolutely LOVE their spicy Szechuan stir-fry sauce and when it is on sale, will buy ten bottles at a time. It is very spicy and flavored absolutely perfectly. I use their classic stir-fry sauce for my children's stir-fry, as the spicy Szechuan is indeed too spicy for them. I don't care for the Saigon Sizzle, which you like, as it is too sweet for me, and I only like sweetness in my desserts. If you like spicy, try the Szechuan spicy stir-fry if you haven't already . . . delicious . . . Have you tried it?

■ By Lorione on November 1, 2008 11:10 P.M.

I have long been a fan of the rice cooker. My stepfather is Japanese-American and I was raised eating rice from a rice cooker with just about every meal. I remember seeing ads for instant rice that advertised that it never stuck together, and thinking, "That's weird, isn't rice supposed to stick together?" Anyway, when I got my first apartment in college, the first appliance I wanted was a rice cooker. It was far more important than a toaster. That Christmas, my parents got me a Hitachi Chime-O-Matic with an On and Warm setting. That was over twenty years ago, and I've used that very same one several times a week ever since. Unlike the dire warnings you have seen, my instruction booklet actually comes with directions for steaming veggies! (Mine has a little steamer insert that is basically a little raised disk with holes that goes in the bottom before you add veggies and water.) I have to admit, I have never tried cooking a protein in it. I will have to try that! I wonder if you could start with the flash-frozen boneless, skinless chicken breasts, or if you'd need to thaw them first?

EBERT: Best to thaw them first.

■ **By Shawn on November 1, 2008 11:51 P.M.**

Minute Rice in the rice cooker? Didn't that "very quickly" turn into mush? :) I'm reading your blog for the first time, interesting stuff!

EBERT: No, because *the Pot knows.*

■ **By Eleanor on November 2, 2008 12:26 A.M.**

What's this I read about rinsing the rice three times? Is that before or after cooking? I've never rinsed rice in my life. I'm a streamlined, prep-to-table-better-be-at-most-an-hour kind of girl. Rinse rice? What say you, O Rice Guru?

EBERT: Before. For me, that's optional.

■ **By Jen on November 2, 2008 1:12 A.M.**

How great to see your post! I run a hotel front desk at night and go to school, and my little rice Pot has been my best friend for years. Lack of money, time, space, energy, or ideas—if you have the rice Pot, you're good to go. I have carried it across country and back multiple times in multiple cars and it's become one of my most cherished possessions.

■ **By Michael on November 2, 2008 1:41 A.M.**

I've been thinking about buying a rice cooker for a few weeks. I'm curious what size cooker would be best for a single guy? Three cups?

EBERT: Three cups, unless you want to cook batches for later.

■ **By CK on November 2, 2008 5:46 A.M.**

Besides cooking up oatmeal, soups, and stews, how about using the rice cooker to poach fish or eggs? Maybe adding a small colander or folding metal basket might enable the rice cooker to work as a steamer, too. Would be interesting to see if it's possible to steam-cook a cake or quiche.

EBERT: Can be done. Some of them come with a little insert for holding an egg.

■ By Devin Chalmers on November 2, 2008 6:18 A.M.

I've had luck putting a hand towel over the little hole in the top of the Pot while it cooks. Keeps down spatter, but lets out enough steam to cook the rice anyway. (After it switches to "warm" you should certainly do this to keep the nice warm moist air in.) Also you might be trying to cook too much rice. I never fill mine more than halfway, mostly.

■ By Robert of Taoyuan City, Taiwan, on November 2, 2008 7:47 A.M.

Roger, I buy these organic broccoli florets that come in packs. I take a handful out, wash them a bit, and just throw them on top of my rice while it's on Warm inside the rice cooker (the veggie cooks in about twenty minutes, coming out still green and fresh-looking). Very convenient, no need to steam them separately. I also reheat my overnight viands this way, to take to work as a packed lunch, or what we call "bien-dang."

■ By Kathleen on November 2, 2008 10:24 A.M.

I need you to tell me this: Will the Pot cook my rice until it's done and then turn off to Warm where I live, here at nearly 5,000 feet above sea level? If you tell me it will, I promise to order the Pot. The only reason I haven't is that I've doubted it would know when rice (or dried beans) is done at this altitude because (if I could phrase this as a question, I would call this a trick question) at this altitude, whole grain rice and dried beans never do finish cooking. I don't want to hassle with a pressure cooker, and I'm a whole grain kind of gal, so I live with unsatisfactory brown rice and sort of crunchy dried beans. Can you assure me that this miracle device, the Pot, will solve my high-altitude cooking problems?

EBERT: It worked for me as expected in Park City, Utah, elevation 7,000 feet.

■ By Grant on November 2, 2008 11:58 A.M.

I got one of these a few years ago. My first thought was, "Why the hell didn't I know about these when I was living on mac 'n' cheese and ramen noodles?"

To the people who don't want to risk the money, spend the fifteen or twenty bucks at Target (or K-Mart or whatever). It's totally worth it.

And I know Ebert already answered the guy who asked what size to get, but the sizes are listed for UNCOOKED rice. So a three-cup cooker will have about nine cups of cooked rice. Do the math on a sixteen-cup cooker. Too much rice for a single guy!

Thank you, Roger. Knowing that your Pot performed as expected at 7,000 feet, I have, as promised, ordered the Pot.

**■ By Dennis Freire on November 2, 2008
6:22 P.M.**

My rice cooker was indispensable the years I lived in Japan.

In Japan I cooked rice in it, of course. In the morning I used it to make hot rice to eat with nato. In the evening for the meal's rice. I also made miso soup in it. I cooked cracked wheat in it when I wanted an American-style breakfast. I warmed up cabbage and onions in it, steamed hakusai cabbage or Chinese broccoli. I made a Chinese dish called mama-dofu—kind of a spicy sauce with lots of tofu in it.

We got one for a wedding present here in the States. It was the best gift and lasted much longer than the cash we got at the reception.

My daughter is moving to Germany in December. She'll live in a small apartment with no counter space. Now I know what I'm getting her for Christmas.

**■ By Shane on November 3, 2008
1:01 A.M.**

I must mention that once, by mistake, my girlfriend tossed the rice into the cooker without the metal lining in place. I had to unscrew the bottom array and shake each grain out, but I marveled at the simplicity and functionality of the rice cooker's inner workings. On, Warm, and Off. If only everything in life could be so clear. (Incidentally, my girlfriend swears by the expensive Japanese rice found at upscale markets. You *can* taste the difference.) She also told me her grandmother would quote a popular Japanese aphorism: "Don't disturb the rice, even if the baby is crying." I suppose by that she means that one shouldn't lift the lid, stir, or do anything once the rice is simmering. This explains why my fussed-over stove-top rice always used to turn out like gruel. It's not surprising that I've never seen my gf cook rice with anything but her trusty rice cooker (she got it free with her Honda). Another point worth mentioning: Japanese restaurants that make rice in the old stone Pots make a rice so wonderful, your faith in your trusty cooker may diminish. It's also common knowledge that rice should be washed. Just put the rice in the cooker liner, fill it with water, swish it around with a clean hand, and pour out the water. Repeat until the water runs clear. It's a technique like panning for gold. Then do it with filtered water a time or two if you don't trust your local water department (and who should?).

Yes, I, your constant reader, recalled your aunt Mary's extra helping "for fear of company" recipe, although I'll be damned if I can remember the context in which you first mentioned it. I believe it was within the last two years that I read it, but hyperlinks to such arcana would be appreciated.

■ By JJM on November 3, 2008 1:04 P.M.
This took me back to my undergrad years when I was in Japan.

A typical girls' dorm room had a rice cooker, a hot pot (strictly for boiling water, although soup and hot dogs also worked), and a toaster oven.

A really nice room would have had a rice cooker, hot pot, toaster oven, an electric skillet, and maybe a microwave.

These were all against school fire safety policies. It really is amazing what kind of meals we could make, including miso shiru from scratch.

I later lived in apartments or was invited to apartments where all they had was a rice cooker and an electric skillet and sometimes a hibachi. We steamed pot stickers and buns (nikuman or baozi).

Traditional Japanese homes do not have ovens, so baking was sort of a challenge. I did manage to make banana bread by steaming.

My last time in Japan, I don't quite remember how, but I did make a turkey stew, cranberry sauce, tapioca pudding, wild rice stuffing. I don't think I used the hibachi. That was a Japanese Thanksgiving, of course.

Last time I used a rice cooker, it was to make rice for sushi. I always add a quarter to a third of brown rice and then toasted sesame seeds for added nutrition and taste. I prefer honey instead of sugar.

Growing up, I learned how to cook rice in a regular pot—without butter. Rice should stick together if it's Japanese style.

Now, I prefer bread from scratch. I have my own bread maker. I understand I can use it to make jam. Mostly, I like to make marmalade from scratch. I understand I can use my bread maker for that. I tried my Crock-Pot, but that didn't work. Maybe I can use my rice cooker for that.

EBERT: Love those toasted sesame seeds! We have a bread maker, which can be timed to awaken us with the aroma of fresh-baked cinnamon bread. A confession: The Pot may be all you need, but it needn't be all you want. As every realtor will tell you, nothing smells more like home than cinnamon.

■ By Grant on November 3, 2008 2:24 P.M.
Any idiot can make good rice using a simple rice cooker, but it takes a special kind of idiot, such as me, to screw it up. In an attempt to make the meal even healthier, I used filtered water with the rice. Unfortunately the water came from my Brita pitcher straight from the refrigerator, and apparently near-frozen water has a way of tricking

the cooker into thinking it is prematurely done. I still use filtered water with my rice, but now I let it warm to room temperature before cooking.

■ By Niki on November 3, 2008 4:28 P.M.

My boyfriend brings up the idea of getting a rice cooker periodically, but I always shoot it down because I have never had any trouble making rice. (My method for white rice such as basmati or jasmine: Place 2:1 water: rice in a covered saucepan over high heat. As soon as the water is boiling—you should be able to see the lid rattling, but I have been known to lift and take a quick peek—immediately drop your burner to the lowest setting it can handle. Wait about ten minutes for one cup of rice, fifteen for two to three cups. Take a very quick peek, and if you see a few "holes" in the mass of rice—due to escaping steam—remove the rice from the heat. The step of knowing when rice is finished is tricky, but once the upper grains are clearly dry you can risk letting steam escape while you take a fork and probe the bottom of the pan. If you want to err on the side of caution, remove the rice from the heat while there is still a bit of water in the pan and leave the lid on so steaming will continue while you prepare your other food.

The problem with stove-top rice is that you have to keep your mind on it. When you have kids and writing deadlines and other distractions, a rice cooker does sound nice. I thought I was saving money by keeping myself tethered to the stove (since I couldn't argue that rice from a Pot would be better than my own rice), but now you have shown me the light: I can cook many things in a steamer, and free myself up to write until I'm damn well ready to deal with the food again. The possibilities seem endless.

I'm still quite confused about some of the recipes (if I am putting raw meat in with the rice and veggies, does the meat go in after the rice is done or somewhere in the middle? Do the veggies go on top of the raw meat or later? Also, when I cook on the stove-top, I like to sauté in order to get oil and seasonings into my mushrooms, and I can't tell if the Pot will achieve a similar result via steaming), but I figure I'll go check out some of those cookbooks you mention to see if they'll give me some more detailed guidance.

Ebert: Things go in by reverse order of how much cooking time you think they need.

■ By Davie Michael Bennett on November 3, 2008 6:03 P.M.

I would love to hear your thoughts and suggestions for avoiding the horrible scourge of Scorched Pot Bottom. I have the Panasonic ten-cup, and I have never not lost a small handful of rice at the bottom of my Pot. I've tried oil, nonstick cooking spray, more water, less water, prayer, and pleading. Any wise words from the Pot guru?

EBERT: My Pots have never scorched, not once. Are you using enough liquid? The Pot should turn off before that happens.

■ By Dana on November 3, 2008 8:38 P.M.
After so many thoughtful and delicious posts, I hesitate to add my two cents' worth, but here goes: Recently I found out that you can put leftover rice in one of those Ziploc bags, then freeze it.

OK, that is not the exciting part. Hear me out.

Later on, as it might be for lunch the next day, you can fish out that bag, put a little water in it if it looks dry at all, and then microwave it for about a minute until it's hot. And it's really good. It isn't all sort of weird and dry the way rice gets if you leave it in the fridge. I should say that I've only tried this with basmati, my table rice of choice if I'm not eating East Asian food.

Give it a try. And I will buy a Zojirushi rice cooker—I love my Zojirushi bread machine.

■ By Cabir on November 4, 2008 1:41 A.M.
This was fascinating, but also all true. As a person raised in the West but now living in India, I have two Pots—one by Morphy Richards and one by Black and Decker—and they both cost around the same. In fact, they look spectacular—the Morphy Richards especially has this amazing steel sheen to it—almost futuristic.

I must state here that I do not use any other cooking utensils than the Pots. Why? They're easy, convenient, and you can actually whip up fancy meals with these, once you spend time getting to know them. For example, I make the BEST bacon and cheese frittata using the Pot, even better than in any other equipment I've used. They do omelets spectacularly, and they boil water at lightning-fast speed. Seriously, I never saw water boil that quickly.

What is especially nice is when I leave for a long day at work—I just put in a couple pounds of chicken on the bone, cover it with water, add some seasoning, and let it cook. Since it switches to Keep Warm automatically, I am treated to a spectacularly delicious meal when I get home around ten hours later. In this aspect it does rival Crock-Pot cooking.

Rice cooks perfectly, potatoes cook perfectly, and since all Pots usually have nonstick bottoms, you can cook virtually anything, or fry anything, without worrying about cleaning up or making a mess.

Ebert, I do think, though, that this piece of equipment is not just meant for solitary writers or single people on a budget. On the contrary, my own demographic is removed from this, and I have specifically chosen the Pot to replace my traditional pans and woks and frying pans, only because it does the work of ALL of that equipment, plus more.

Thanks, Roger, for making this divine piece of technology better known in the West. I was afraid it would remain an Eastern secret for far too long! If you can, seek out a Chinese brand called Koryo—they make the BEST Pots, not much to look at, but they LAST, and their cooking times are always on point.

■ By Qui Lam on November 4, 2008 5:50 A.M.

The principle of the rice cooker is like that of the toaster. First, you push down the button. The heater element then reaches a certain high degree for some length of time. After the rice has absorbed all the water (the Vietnamese measure the water level by the third phalange of the middle finger from the rice) and the heater element has reached a certain point, the heat inside will either be cut off or lowered down to a minimal level depending on which button you hit—Off or Keep Warm.

■ By Dave Alkema on November 4, 2008 3:08 P.M.

I'm fairly skeptical of this magical Pot that you speak of. I lived for more than two years with nothing but the smallest of all the George Foreman grills and a hot plate. There wasn't a single thing I couldn't do with those things. If I have a chance, though, I may pick up one of these rice cookers and see if there's anything I can do with it on my very limited budget. Thanks for the advice!

EBERT: Unlike the hot plate, you can walk away from it, take a shower, walk the dog, and read the paper and your house doesn't burn down.

■ By Glenn Fawcett on November 4, 2008 5:05 P.M.

Thanks for the nonrice ideas! As for how the magic Pot works, it's just like that old science demo where you put some water in an unwaxed paper cup and hold it over a candle. The water boils but the cup doesn't burn until it boils dry. In a rice cooker, once the moisture is gone, a bimetallic strip (invented by the great English clock maker John Harrison) bends with increased temperature and flips the cooker over to Warm mode. Simple and elegant.

EBERT: Wrong! It's an occult mystery.

■ **By Kathleen on November 8, 2008 11:24 A.M.**

Roger, I bought the Pot. You were right. It does work here at 4,700 feet. I was astonished at the much higher proportion of water to rice that it called for in contrast to what's recommended on the whole grain rice packaging. It cooked for about an hour and ten minutes, shut itself off, and I let it sit for another ten minutes. Perfect, fluffy rice. For the first time since I moved to this altitude, perfect, fluffy rice. Thanks, Roger!

■ **By Paulo on November 15, 2008 6:49 A.M.**

Roger, I don't have a proper kitchen, so I use my Pot to cook pasta, rice, and lentils. The only bad thing about the Pot is that it is limited to boiling. This means that you can't create the fried base of onions and garlic that classic soups usually have. Apart from that, the Pot is perfect. I couldn't live without it.

EBERT: I have done this. Spray the Teflon Pot with low-fat Pam (olive oil type). Add a little olive oil and chopped onions and garlic. Close and heat. Don't allow the onions to burn. You can open briefly to stir the onions a little and check on the progress. Monitor closely, and have the other soup ingredients all ready to add.

■ **By Molly L on December 4, 2008 7:17 A.M.**

. . . I love our rice cooker, too! We once went camping for two full months and cooked most of our breakfasts and dinners out of our rice cooker.

However, due to the amount of cooking we do on it, we invested in a fuzzy logic Zojirushi. Not only can it cook brown rice very well (which our old one can't do), it has a much-loved, much-used feature: the timer. For blood sugar reasons I have to eat within about twenty minutes of waking up. My Zojirushi is timed so that every day I have slow-cooked oatmeal waiting for me upon waking. And it's great to set up rice cooking in the morning, with it timed to be done at dinner. My rice cooker has two timers, actually, so I have one automatically set for breakfast and one for dinnertime.

They are expensive, but I actually worked out the price for buying the rice cooker and cooking with cheap organic oatmeal versus the cereal we'd been eating every day—and the cooker paid for itself quickly.

It might be worth mentioning the timing feature in your Pot book. Some folks may not think a Pot is worth it if they have to set it after coming home from work in the evenings. The only drawback about the timer is the annoyingly cheery "twinkle theme" that plays when it's finished. My husband opened it up and removed the speaker.

At the risk of revealing the man behind the curtain, the rice cooker is actually very simple technologically. There is a thermostat that touches the bottom of the Pot that switches off (or to Warm) when all the water has boiled off. This prevents the rice from burning. This is a great convenience because, as others have noted here, you can make rice on the stove but you have to mind it.

Since the boiling stops when the water is gone, the main thing that controls the softness of the grains is the ratio of water to rice (or other ingredients like oatmeal). There is also the slight complication that the rice in the Pot needs to be deep; that is, a ten-cup cooker works best with seven to ten cups but would not work well with only three cups.

While it is in cooking mode, the rice maker is the same as any electric pot. So, you can make pasta in a rice cooker (though you cannot cook rice with a pasta maker!).

■ By Kathleen Kakacek on May 25, 2009 2:11 P.M.

I want you to know how much I'm enjoying the rice cooker you recommended. It isn't fussy and it makes perfect rice every time here at 4,700 feet above sea level. I've recently discovered basmati rice, and really like the texture. My husband and I have rediscovered the joys of eating rice, after thirty-some years at this altitude, and we have you to thank! How's the cookbook coming? I don't have any recipes to contribute, but I can tell you that following the instructions that came with the cooker gives me perfectly cooked dried beans and whole grain rice. My husband tells me just about every weekend how glad he is that we bought the cooker. Just thought you'd like to know.

■ By HopeB on July 1, 2009 3:53 P.M.

I have one question: Will it cook grits?

Not those terrible impostors, the so-called instant grits or even the dreaded quick grits, but honest-to-God, stone-ground, tender, yummy, real grits?

Because that would be awesome.

EBERT: No problem. (See recipe on page 98.)

■ By misterbeets on August 7, 2009 8:51 P.M.

As I understand it, a rice cooker monitors temperature. Once the water boils off and the temperature begins to rise above 212°F, it switches to Warm.

EBERT: Aw . . . you gave away the secret!

Glad to see someone who actually uses the rice cooker for other things aside from just rice. I've never really gotten around to experimenting with it yet, aside from trying my hand at making congee. As a college student, however, being able to toss in a frozen fish and adding an egg and soy sauce have proven to be quite handy with rice, among other delicious alternatives.

Zojirushi's fancy rice cookers are actually quite spectacular. My mom has only just upgraded our rice cooker from the previous one (ten years strong from almost DAILY use). I've seen wondrous things concocted. I have to ask my mom, but one of the things she makes quite well is steamed fried rice. I have to ask her for the exact recipe, but it involves chopped duck and liver sausage, shiitake mushrooms, bok choy, and some type of sauce. To be continued . . .

EBERT: Got to have that recipe!

AMUSING

■ By Rhett McNeil on November 1, 2008 7:25 P.M.

It seems to me that the rice cooker way of life you endorse would be perfect for the stars of the documentary *Cinemaniacs*. Makes sense, since it was developed by a borderline cinemaniac (I mean that in the best sense, of course). Also, Werner Herzog could probably have used these techniques to make that leather shoe a little bit more digestible, no? Thanks so much for the years of reviews and the new joys of the blog. Happy rice cookering!

■ By Tiffany Sears on November 1, 2008 7:45 P.M.

Ebert, I could not love your blog any more than I do. I clicked on the link expecting some dry reference from a Pot to . . . I don't know, the latest Kevin Smith movie, and was surprised, hesitant, disappointed, humored, and then informed. I think I'm actually gonna go out and get one of these things now. Thanks, and keep up my favorite blog (you pushed out DailyKos, can you believe it?).

■ By DigicamLife on November 1, 2008 7:52 P.M.

Cooking humor? Who knew? We have a cooker. Have had it for at least ten years. Used it maybe five times early on. Been in the barn ever since. I liked your take, so tomorrow I will pull it out of the cabinet and give it another chance. Luckily I passed on selling it on eBay.

So who has the #1 Best Written Blog on the Internet?

EBERT: Dan Lyons at http://realdanlyons.com /blog/. I'm happy being down here at #2. It takes the pressure off. The whole list is here: http://www.computerworld.com/action/ article.do?command=viewArticleBasic &articleId=9116838&&source=NLT_ AM&nlid=1.

■ By Kim, Australia, on November 1, 2008 9:45 P.M.

When the wedding wrap revealed a rice cooker, I put on my best at-least-it's-not-another-platter smile. Three years on, the husband's gone but the rice cooker is still with me. Steamed veggies, quick risottos, and perfect basmati every time.

■ By Joel on November 1, 2008 10:27 P.M.

First off, I must say that the rice cooker my wife and I received for our wedding was, hands down, the best present we got—beating out the TV and the queen-sized bed.

■ By Eric L. on November 1, 2008 10:28 P.M.

Reading this while watching an Iron Chef (Japan) rerun left over on my TiVo, I notice that one of them has a Pot going. If it's good enough for an Iron Chef, it should be good enough for all of us, no?

■ By UPN on November 2, 2008 12:44 A.M.

Just one question—when you are pulling off your culinary feats, where on your person do you hide Remy?! . . . Anyway, when I tried the rice cooker adventure inspired by you, imagine my surprise when the first spoonful suddenly made my mind zoom back to the good ole days when I staggered home bone-tired from hectic play and Mom would comfort me with a ready plate of thumping good grains!

You may also be interested to know that rice cookers and Indian films have a faithful connection. Last year I watched a pale derivative of *Lolita* starring the famous Amitabh

Bacchan, and in one sequence, the errant husband tries to make conversation with his wife in the kitchen—she's silent but the rice cooker gives off an aggressive hiss! I thought this was a neat idea until a critic pointed out that this was clichéd usage!

■ By Robert of Taoyuan City, Taiwan, on November 2, 2008 8:12 A.M.

Um, Roger . . . where did you get minotaur meat for your stew? I tried asking around a Cretan market today, but all I got from the people there were wide-eyed stares of disbelief. One of the vendors even hurled a basket of Rotten Tomatoes at me, opprobriously calling me a "potty" (you know, it's funny that she should use that word . . .). Of course, a fracas ensued immediately afterward, and more tomatoes. The whole market was thrown into turmoil.

EBERT: Quiet! It's a protected species. Tastes like chicken.

■ By smrana on November 2, 2008 9:29 A.M.

Turning to the snakier, murkier realities, and as an individual who would fit into more than one of the subcategories listed in paragraph number 1 of the above, namely one cornered to cook now and then, who would be more than content to devote less time and energy to the same, I really wonder how a device (ref almighty Wiki) comprising a heating element, a thermostat—I hope you know what that is—and a Pot—excuse me—can function as a combination of Houdini and Aladdin. Does it really?—short of being a devotee and convert to the gospel of the Pot—if that is permitted—(perhaps the brilliance lies in the simplicity).

■ By A. M. Anderson on November 2, 2008 10:26 A.M.

When my husband and I first married, sixteen years ago, I wanted to buy a rice cooker. Like the United Nations, we shared veto power and he used it. (The Swiss don't spend money they don't have.) But that started me on the path I am on today. I adapted and even thrived in my quest to grasp the elusive secret of rice cooking.

When I traveled to Japan, I was the houseguest of a very gracious woman who attempted to teach me the secrets of rice cooking, albeit in Japanese, but to no avail. I carried on with my quest. Through the years I've attained a certain proficiency to the point where my failures are also satisfying in an odd way.

It has been at least ten years now that my husband has attempted to buy me a rice cooker on a biyearly basis. It never makes it to the cash register. I would certainly miss my encounters with the rice, water, fire, and salt. I want to know what the Pot knows.

■ By smrana on November 2, 2008 12:04 P.M.

Are you suggesting the Pot is to cooking what the wheel is to machinery?

EBERT: Are you?

■ By Matt Kaufman on November 2, 2008 7:44 P.M.

Urbana born, Potomac bred, I had never even HEARD of a rice cooker until I was twenty-two and in college, when I met my Taiwanese-born wife. When I introduced her to my parents, they did their best to make her feel welcome by serving the only rice-based dish they knew—pork chops, with cream of mushroom gravy on Minute Rice. She was appalled—APPALLED—by the Minute Rice, but didn't let it show. To this day, a rice cooker has served as the mainstay of our lineup of kitchen appliances. I don't get to eat as many potatoes as I'd like (Irish/German), but well-made rice is like wonder-starch—you can do anything with it.

But stay away from Minute Rice if you can—for the widest selection of quality rice (and rice cookers) in the Chicago area, my wife recommends Mitsuwa Grocery in Arlington Heights, on Algonquin and Arlington Heights Road—go for the groceries, stay for the many Chinese/Japanese food counters in the food court.

■ **By smrana on November 2, 2008 8:09 P.M.**

The potato poem is another gem which points to the beauties of the life less encumbered—I always love Van Gogh's painting of his "Room." In fact, I have a small print of it hanging in my own place—just a bed and a table and a towel hanging from the peg. I once visited Mahatma Gandhi's place of detention in the Agha Khan palace in Pune in Western India—his possessions amounted to his wooden footwear, spectacles, his favorite Bhagavad Gita, and another item or two. Even films are valuable insofar as they enable us to explore and polish the grandeur of the inner universe, which is the common heritage of a human being. The Pot, which you have so eloquently and poetically described, also has a certain austere technological and utilitarian beauty with its relative simplicity like the Pots of olden times. Long live Pots!

■ **By Mark on November 2, 2008 8:13 P.M.**

I stopped eating meat a year ago. You know how I feel now? Bored. Dullest thing I ever decided to do. Oh sure, my health is better, I've lost weight, I look younger, can exercise more—so I'm a real healthy boring bore. I don't have the snap left to even put in a more interesting modifier for "bore" than "boring."

And the rice cooker is my pal, too.

What's struck me over the last year, after I had my taste buds and wit removed, is that there is no need to spend a lot on food. If you're willing to eat dried legumes and rice, the world is—well, if not your oyster, let's nod toward Val Kilmer and say it's your huckleberry, or daisy, or whatever other piece of flora he was spouting off about as he coughed up parts of his lung in *Tombstone*. But I'm serious about the dried beans and other grains. Cheap as can be, nutritious, and even a lunkhead like me can soak beans overnight.

You know—and this is none of my business, so feel free to tell me to screw off if it's too personal—but how have your dietary habits changed since the surgery? You mentioned that you haven't tasted food for more than a year. I'm with you on that as well. Anosmia, they tell me mine's called. Better than anhedonia, I guess. I've laid off things that might spoil in a secret way, like milk, which looks OK. I can't tell 'til it's coming back up that it's no good. More than that, I eat as much chile pepper and curry as I can get my hands on, as that sweaty reaction is something close to taste.

Thanks for not sending me off to Williams-Sonoma for some fancy-dancy thing. I hate being in there as much as I hate waiting in Victoria's Secret, her secret being that no one cares how the present's wrapped, so long as there's easy access.

EBERT: I haven't eaten a bite for two years. I give myself liquid nourishment through a G-tube. Thus I have been a perfect vegetarian without a single slip for twenty-four months, on low fat and low salt. Today my cholesterol is 145 over something, my blood pressure is low normal, and I have never felt more clear-minded or zestful.

■ By Tony Sosa on November 3, 2008 12:34 P.M.

I'm going to need a second rice cooker to try these experiments. My Chinese wife would stab me to death with her chopsticks if I attempted any of this with her prized possession. It's nice to see whimsy in your posts, Roger.

EBERT: Ooooo! Didn't Takshi Kitano kill someone like that? In the eyeballs. I hate it when that happens.

■ By Junior Wences on November 3, 2008 1:10 P.M.

Finally, Roger Ebert breaks his thirty-year silence on rice cookers! Now that he's showing his cards, I'd love to hear his thoughts on the Foreman Grill and teen pregnancy!

EBERT: The Foreman Grill! Ah! Even for grilled *asperge*. Teen pregnancy: Use the Pot instead of sex.

■ By Red Beans and Rice on November 3, 2008 1:52 P.M.

. . . as to Tony Sosa's post and your response . . . as my wise mother says, "It's all fun and games until someone loses an eye."

■ By Eleanor on November 3, 2008 7:02 P.M.

OK, I'm sold. You'd be a demon on QVC or HSN, Roger, even with your primitive sign language. Santa (me) is bringing this for Christmas. I've never used Minute Rice (I had a Wacky Pack as a kid that had a pic of "Minute Lice" and that did it for me), but tell me this: Do I need to rinse good old Uncle Ben's before I cook it in the Pot? I've never rinsed UB's in my life, but I'm open to new things. Ha. And now I'm lusting after a bread maker! God help me if you talk about cars . . .

EBERT: Forget about rinsing rice. What you need is the turbocharged 1957 Studebaker Golden Hawk.

■ By Paul Arrand Rodgers on November 3, 2008 8:33 P.M.

For shame, Roger—you turn down millions of dollars from Mayor McCheese and his roving gang of happy, child-pleasing artery cloggers, but you happily take money from the Amazon.com rice-cooking lobby?

I have a friend who has a rice cooker. Until this post, I thought they were stupid, useless things. This friend got the micro-zirconium, fuzzy logic, happy song–playing things. I ate at his house once and waited (and waited and waited) for the food because he insisted upon hearing the happy song.

Now that I find these things are one touch and wonderful, I find my college has banned them! Dumb question, but is it worth it to sneak one in? Food here on the weekends is notoriously awful, and the cooker would come in a plain old box. It would be easy . . .

EBERT: Maybe this is not the kind of Pot they banned?

■ By T. Ladner on November 3, 2008 8:44 P.M.

To persuade Mrs. Ebert on your book title, show her these:
Crit, or Get Off the Pot
If the Pot Smokes, You're Doing It Wrong
Roger Ebert's Overlooked Rice Papers
Peace in. Peace out.

EBERT: The Perfect London Pot? A Pot Is Just a Pot? Pot in the Dark? The Movie Pot Man? Roger Ebert's 4-Star Pot? Behind the Pot's Mask? Ebert's Pot Yearbook 2008? Two Weeks in the Midday Pot? The Great Pots? The Great Pots II? Pot by Ebert? War and Pot? You Can't Go to Pot Again? Gone with the Pot? I'm busy, I'm busy!

■ By T. Ladner on November 3, 2008 10:25 P.M.

It's My Pot and It Freaks Me Out
I Like Pot by Ebert
Ebert's Pot Yearbook 2009.

EBERT: Oh my God, Ronnie! You're a Pot! You've been a Pot all along!

■ By Robert of Taoyuan City, Taiwan, on November 3, 2008 10:29 P.M.

If I might add, Roger . . .

David CopperPot	Harry Potter (. . . no, erase this)
Pot & Prejudice	School of Pot
Of Pots and Men	Nosferatu the Pot
Potty & Pottier	Kind Pots and Coronets
Pot Wars	Dead Pots Society
Robopot	Around the World in Potty Days
Lady Chatterley's Potter	Dr. Strangelove, Or: How I Learned to Stop Worrying and Love the Pot

■ By Paul Arrand Rodgers on November 3, 2008 11:17 P.M.

Oh, no, *the* Pot is banned here at the College of Mount St. Joseph, as are all electronic cooking devices, minus the school-supplied microwaves in the lobbies; evil, monolithic relics of a bygone age where Hungry-Man dinners were considered a good decision.

To quote:

"Toasters, toaster ovens, microwave ovens, George Foreman grills (or similar versions), popcorn poppers are not permitted. A kitchenette, equipped with a microwave, is available on each floor."

It says nothing of rice cookers, but surely if they're against knocking out the fat, they're against the Pot.

What to do?

EBERT: Switch schools.

■ By Dan W., Owosso, MI, on November 4, 2008 4:26 A.M.

Rog: Aside from movies, I have not read a topic from you that you are so passionate about other than Steak N Shake restaurants. You are the proverbial peeling onion, each layer revealing another facet of your life experience that I cannot avoid reading, for fear of missing another classic sentence or observation that compels me to say to my wife, "You've got to read what Ebert wrote today!" I'm off to purchase my Pot. While viewing the many models to choose from, I will adhere to the credo "WWED."

EBERT: Uh, WWED?

Naive and humble one . . . it stands for: What Would Ebert Do?

■ By Robert of Taoyuan City, Taiwan, on November 4, 2008 5:18 A.M.

Dear Roger, here's a limerick I thought of during my leisure time:
Mr. & Mrs. Pot
My next door neighbors Mr. and Mrs. Pot,
Whose sex lives are way over the top!
From night till morning,
It's BANG CLANG BOOMING!
Will somebody please ring for a cop!

■ By Robert of Taoyuan City, Taiwan, on November 4, 2008 6:13 A.M.

Lonely Mabel
   There was a lonely Pot named Mabel,
   Who cried night after night to a bundle.
   Until came a pan,
   By the name of Dan.
   But alas! He was a pan with no handle!

EBERT:
   A Pot that was named Sarah Jane
   Achieved a measure of fame
   By tipping its cooker
   Like a flatulent hooker
   And tooting out "Lili Marlene."

■ By Chuck, Bellingham, WA, on November 4, 2008 3:13 P.M.

Thanks, Roger—very serendipitous. Our trusty rice cooker's timer crapped out a couple of months ago after about fourteen years. I was occasionally remembering to have a look at rice cookers when in various stores, but all of them had way too many features, were too big, or something else equally grotesque.

So my order went in yesterday, and the big brown truck will deliver the new Pot tomorrow morning. With just two settings it will fit right in with my cooking credo—when the smoke alarm goes off, it's done.

■ **By Anne on November 9, 2009 8:49 P.M.**
Upon discovering this wonderful thread, I pulled out my never-used rice cooker and immediately cooked two meals with it. Perfect! Thanks for the inspiration. Oh, and the fact that my microwave just bit the dust has absolutely nothing to do with it.

Ebert: Well, of course not.

14

NONVEGETARIAN RECIPES

Note: For all recipes with rice
All recipes with rice are measured with the cup that comes with the rice cooker. This cup is essentially ¾ U.S. measuring cup dry rice.

NONVEGETARIAN CHILI

ROGER'S FAVORITE CHILI RECIPE

■ **By qdpsteve on November 1, 2008 9:55 P.M.**

Apologies in advance but I have to ask: What's your fave rice cooker recipe for chili?

EBERT: Just how you'd figure: beans, ground or chunk beef or vegetable protein, onions, garlic. That's basic. Then maybe some peppers, maybe some bacon, maybe some cocoa powder, tomatoes or try stewed tomatoes (bigger tomato chunks cut up), and chili powder, garam masala, or the hot peppers of your choice.

JERRY'S CHILI *Serves 8*

■ **By Jerry Roberts, Birmingham, Alabama, on January 5, 2009 8:03 P.M.**

Based on some advice given on your blog, I have finally figured out how to get my rice cooker to work without having to wipe water off the crown molding.

I've been working with some things such as taking my chili recipe out of the Dutch oven and trying it in the rice cooker and it is delicious. I don't know if you can eat chili but here's my recipe anyway:

Ingredients:

- 2 pounds ground round
- 2 teaspoons Tabasco sauce
- ½ cup water
- 1 garlic clove, minced
- 1 teaspoon pepper
- 1 tablespoon Italian seasoning
- 1 tablespoon olive oil
- 1 medium onion, chopped
- 1½ teaspoons ground cumin
- 2 teaspoons salt
- 2 cans kidney beans, drained
- 2 cans (14.5 ounces each) whole tomatoes, drained and chopped
- 4 tablespoons chili powder (I use 6 but only when I am the only one eating it)

Method:

1. Brown the ground round in a skillet and drain.
2. Sauté onions in olive oil in the rice cooker.
3. Combine with all the remaining ingredients in a rice cooker and mix thoroughly.
4. Put on Warm and cook for 8 to 10 hours.
5. Stir occasionally (optional; varying results have occurred).

NONVEGETARIAN GRAINS

RICE COOKER MUSHROOM RISOTTO *Prep Time: 15 minutes, serves 4 to 6*

■ **By Marie Haws**

Taken from http://www.sunbeam.com.au/Pages/Recipes/RecipeDetail.aspx?iid=9286, this is a delicious risotto cooked in the rice cooker.

Ingredients:
2 tablespoons olive oil
⅓ cup butter
1 onion, finely chopped
1 garlic clove, crushed
2 cups uncooked Arborio rice
1 cup dry white wine
4 cups chicken stock, hot
6 ounces Portobello mushrooms, sliced
8 ounces button mushrooms, sliced
½ cup grated Parmesan cheese
¼ cup chopped fresh parsley
Freshly ground black pepper

Method:
1. In a large frying pan, heat half the oil and butter; add the onion and garlic and cook until the onion is tender. Add the rice and stir through to coat the rice with the onion mixture.

2. Add the wine and cook, stirring, until most of the liquid has been absorbed. Transfer the mixture to the rice cooker cooking pan. Add the hot chicken stock and stir through. Making sure that the exterior of the pan is dry, place in the heating vessel.

3. Replace the lid.

4. Depress the automatic control lever to Cook.

5. When the cooking is complete, the lever will automatically switch to the Keep Warm mode. Leave the rice in the cooker for 10 minutes at this stage. DO NOT REMOVE THE LID.

6. Meanwhile, heat the remaining oil and butter in a frying pan, add the mushrooms, and cook, stirring, until the mushrooms are tender; drain any excess liquid.

7. After the rice has been in the Keep Warm mode for 10 minutes, open the lid. Stir in the mushrooms, Parmesan, and parsley. Season to taste with black pepper.

8. Serve immediately.

MACARONI AND CHEESE WITH BACON

■ By Sue Grant, Vancouver Island

Add a little diced bacon to the Pot. Add macaroni and water as directed on the package. Turn on the Pot. When the macaroni is done, drain the water and stir in the cheese and frozen green peas.

NONVEGETARIAN ONE-POT MEALS

SOY RICE AND CHICKEN *Serves 6 to 8*

■ **By Robert of Taoyuan City, Taiwan, on November 2, 2008 6:43 A.M.**

Ingredients:

½ cup Japanese sushi rice
Handful of dried shiitake mushrooms, the
    small variety (if large, cut into strips)
¾ (rice cooker measuring) cup soy sauce

2 tablespoons oil
1 thin slice of gingerroot, cut into thin strips
Handful of chopped, nibble-sized chicken
    pieces, preferably deboned thighs
2 tablespoons soy sauce
3½ cups regular rice

2 tablespoons oil
2 garlic cloves, squashed
½ white onion, sliced into half-rings
3 tablespoons soy sauce
4½ (rice cooker measuring) cups water
Salt

Method:

1. Wash the sushi rice and soak thoroughly in water for half an hour. Put aside.

2. Soak the dried shiitake mushrooms in ¾ cup soy sauce. Put aside (soak until soft).

3. In a nonstick pan, heat 2 tablespoons of oil, then sauté the ginger. Quickly add in the chicken pieces with 2 tablespoons of soy sauce (to give the chicken color). Stir-fry until the chicken is cooked. Set aside on a plate and let cool thoroughly; this is important.

4. Drain the sushi rice of water. Wash the ordinary rice clean and drain of water, too. Remember to drain both rices well.

5. Using your hand, squeeze the shiitake mushrooms of soy sauce, but mind that you do not waste the soy sauce because it will be used afterward.

6. In the selfsame nonstick pan, heat 2 tablespoons of oil. Sauté the garlic, then the onion, and then the mushrooms.

7. Put in all the rice, the sushi and the regular, and also the 3 tablespoons of soy sauce. Stir-fry until the rice is evenly coated with oil and soy. Don't take too long in stir-frying the rice (less than a minute).

8. Pour the rice mixture and the chicken into the rice cooker. Pour in 4½ (rice cooker measuring) cups of water. Also pour in the soy sauce that you used to soak the dried shiitake mushrooms.

9. Add a dash of salt (only a teeny bit).

10. Let stand to cool for about 5 minutes or more, all the while stirring to dissipate the heat. Dissipating the heat is important so as not to mess with the gauging system of your cooker.

11. After cooling, begin to cook the usual way in your rice cooker.

Tips:

1. Remember that by "cup," I refer to the plastic measuring cup that came along with your rice cooker.

2. My father liked to add taro bits to this recipe. This is optional. You may also try canned water chestnuts.

3. Add only a little salt for reasons that are already obvious.

4. Too much sushi rice causes indigestion and constipation. Use only small amounts as I do here, and drink plenty of water.

5. Different brands of soy sauce produce different tastes. It is not advisable to use the Kikkoman brand, as I cannot vouch for the resulting taste, but use the ones that come from Taiwan. These I can vouch for. Remember not to be fooled into buying soy sauce paste. There is a distinction between soy sauce and soy sauce paste.

6. This recipe is actually easier than it looks.

7. Instead of chicken, pork chunks also do well in this recipe. Additional onion, garlic, and ginger aren't out of the question, though one may substitute shallots for the white onion for more pungency. Chopped spring onions may also be fancied. To decrease salinity, go easy on the soy sauce, or use low sodium soy sauce.

CHICKEN AND NOODLES *Serves 6*

■ **By Joe Fricke on November 3, 2008 10:06 A.M.**

I have four boys and a wife. I use the Pot every Sunday. This is what to do. (Note: This recipe requires a larger than 10 cup Pot.)

Method:

1. Purchase a whole chicken, unwrap, and put in the Pot.
2. Add 2 cans chicken broth.
3. Add 1 can cream of chicken soup.
4. Add 1 can cream of mushroom soup.
5. Set to Low.
6. Wait 5 hours.
7. Take the chicken out of the Pot, remove the meat from the bones, and place the meat back in the Pot.
8. Add 1 bag egg noodles.
9. Stir. Wait ½ hour.
10. Eat.

The Pot knows, it understands, it loves.

STEAMED EGGS

■ **By Jane on November 3, 2008 1:44 P.M.**

Whenever I was sick as a child, my mother would mix up some eggs plus a tiny bit of water, and steam the mixture in a rice cooker. You get a soft, fluffy mixture of steamed eggs. It's even better with a bit of soy sauce on top. I just about lived on this after I had my wisdom teeth out.

GARLIC CHICKEN ON FRAGRANT RICE

■ **By John in Calgary on November 4, 2008 9:45 A.M.**

Great as a side dish with stir-fry, chicken, and so on.

Ingredients:

3 cups uncooked jasmine rice
3 cups water
2 tablespoons sesame oil
2 cubes chicken bouillon
⅓ cup olive oil
1 green onion, chopped
2 garlic cloves, smashed
1 (2-inch) piece fresh gingerroot, crushed
1 chicken thigh, cut into ½-inch pieces

Method:

1. Place the rice, water, sesame oil, chicken bouillon, olive oil, green onion, garlic, and ginger in a rice cooker. Stir, then place the chicken on top. Turn on the rice cooker.

2. When the rice is done, mix the rice so that the oil will be evenly mixed with the rice. Serve.

94121 JAMBALAYA *Serves 4 or so*

■ **By jim in SF on January 2, 2009 2:58 P.M.**

If the world were ending tomorrow, I'd still make a rice cooker meal for dinner. The most recent consisted of sautéed onions, andouille sausage, cooked leftover chicken, and bok choy, a sort of 94121 jambalaya.

Ingredients:

½ onion, chopped
Olive oil
3 cups rice
½ cup white wine
3 cups salted water or chicken stock
1 14-ounce sausage, cut into rounds
Bok choy
1 to 2 cups cooked chicken

Additional things you can add:
Worcestershire sauce, Piment d'Espelette or red pepper flakes, anything New Orleans-y such as shrimp or bell pepper

Method:

1. Sauté the onion in olive oil in the Pot.

2. Add the rice and mix in until coated and moist.

3. Throw in some white wine if your wife isn't looking.

4. Add the water or stock to the 3-cup line.

5. Brown 1 sausage, chopped into rounds, separately.

6. After 10 minutes add the bok choy, sausage, and the cooked chicken.

7. The cooker should flip off after 15 minutes or so. Toss the ingredients and let sit another 10 to 15 minutes. Serve.

SEAFOOD JAMBALAYA *Serves 4*

■ **By Jerry Roberts, Birmingham, Alabama, on July 1, 2009 2:37 P.M.**

Ingredients:

- 1 pound shrimp, peeled and deveined
- 1 cup white rice (use the rice cooker measuring cup)
- 1 stick unsalted butter, softened
- 4 ounces mushrooms, sliced
- 8 ounces crabmeat
- 8 ounces beef broth
- 1 medium onion, chopped
- 1 medium bell pepper, chopped

Method:

1. Put all the ingredients into the rice cooker, then turn it on.
2. Cook approximately 30 minutes.
3. Some add drained oysters to the mixture.

CHICKEN SPAGHETTI *Serves 4*

■ **By Jerry Roberts, Birmingham, Alabama, on July 1, 2009 2:37 P.M.**

Ingredients:

- 2 cups spaghetti noodles
- Salt
- 1 cup chopped grilled chicken
- 2 cups pasta sauce
- 1 cup chopped mushrooms
- ½ cup shredded cheese

Method:

1. Snap the spaghetti in half so it will fit into the cooker and cover with water.
2. Add just a dash of salt.
3. Start cooking until the pasta softens.
4. Drain the pasta.
5. Add the chicken, sauce, and mushrooms; stir frequently.
6. Cook 5 minutes.
7. Add the cheese.
8. Stir and serve.

YA YA JAMBALAYA

■ By Paul Arrand Rodgers, on July 2, 2009 8:49 A.M.

Ingredients:

1 cup rice
4 ounces chicken
8 ounces chicken broth
1 can RO*TEL tomatoes
1 medium bell pepper, chopped
1 medium onion, chopped
½ stick unsalted butter
2 teaspoons Cajun seasoning
1 teaspoon Worcestershire sauce
1 teaspoon hot sauce
½ teaspoon salt

Method:

While I guess you could sauté the vegetables or whatever, man up and throw everything in the Pot, mix it together, and start cooking it. If necessary, use water (about ¼ cup) to cover the mixture. You can add sausage, but I'm a college student working in a small dorm room, and smokey links don't sound like something I'd put in jambalaya.

When the rice cooker clicks over, you're swell.

CHICKEN AND THE USUAL SUSPECT VEGETABLES *Serves 6 to 8*

■ By Nels Johnson on July 2, 2009 3:40 P.M.

Chicken and vegetables, adapted from memory of my scoutmaster Dominick Caridi's recipe.

Ingredients:

Rice (cover the bottom of the Pot about a half inch)
Boneless chicken thighs, skinned, cut into ½-inch pieces (I usually have room for 2 or 3)
Black olives, pitted, to taste (the nice ones if you can)
Pearl onions to taste
1 small jar marinated artichoke hearts (use the liquid, too)
1 small jar roasted red peppers, sliced if you like
1 small jar capers, drained
1 can stewed tomatoes, drained
1 small can marinated mushrooms (use the liquid, too)
Vegetable stock, enough to submerge everything (can be cut with water)
A few bay leaves
Optional: Red pepper flakes to taste (to spice it up if you like that)

Method:

Put all the ingredients in the rice cooker and cook until done.

Note:

Feel free to substitute fresh vegetables for canned/jarred if you like. Be sure to add Italian dressing (or similar) to add flavor if marinated artichokes/mushrooms are not used. Just be sure to season it somehow.

SHRIMP AND GRITS À LA RICE COOKER

■ **By Hope B**

Currently I am having a where-have-you-been-all-my-life moment with the very coarsely ground dried corn that some know as grits and some call polenta. Although I use the same basic recipe as polenta, grits have two qualities that I wanted to highlight in their own post—first, their amazing texture when cooked; second, they love to be prepared in the rice cooker.

Use a 1:4 ratio of grits to water with some salt in your rice cooker, and let them sit for 2 hours on the Keep Warm or congee setting after cooking. My favorite way to eat them right now is cold with milk and dark brown sugar for breakfast.

This is based on the Shrimp and Grits recipe by Bill Neal of Crook's Corner in Chapel Hill, NC. They also sell their own grits. He calls for a frying pan. This is the lazy rice cooker way.

Ingredients:
Diced bacon
Peanut oil
Sliced white button mushrooms
Minced scallions
1 garlic clove, peeled and minced
A little lemon juice, Tabasco, salt and pepper,
   and chopped fresh parsley
1 pound fresh shrimp

Method:

About 3.5 to 4 minutes on Cook should be enough for the shrimp. Don't overcook. Quantities? As much as you want, depending on how much you want to make and the size of your Pot.

SALTY RICE WITH TUNA

■ By Chris on August 7, 2009 10:55 P.M.

This is my basic rice recipe that satisfies my craving for something slightly salty, but which is better for you than, say, pizza or a cheeseburger.

Method:

1. Make white rice, but use less water than normal and instead add some soy sauce and a squirt of that spicy red chili sauce in the bottle with the green lid and the Chinese characters on it. (Optionally, you could just make the rice normally and add the sauces later.)

2. At some point while it's cooking, add a drained can of tuna (or don't drain it, whatever).

3. When it's done, sprinkle sesame seeds on top.

4. Eat it. I usually have a salad with no dressing and piece of fruit on the side. Enjoy!

BUBBIE'S TONGUE

■ By Nina Paley on November 1, 2009 8:37 A.M.

When my mom married my dad, he apparently missed his mother's (my bubbie Zelda's) home-cooked tongue. Wanting to please him, my mom sought the recipe from the source. Finally Bubbie Zelda surrendered it, and I share it, in its entirety, with you below:

"Put it in the pot with the ingredients and cook it 'til it's done."

I bet this would work with a rice cooker, too. You're welcome.
P.S. I'm a vegetarian so I've never tried it.

EBERT: I like my tongue with a little English mustard, just like my narwhal.

NONVEGETARIAN SOUPS

■ **By smrana, on November 1, 2008 8:33 P.M.**

Q: Duck Soup?

A: EBERT: Take a duck. Behead it on your boulder. Remove the feathers, wash, chop into pieces, and cover with water and some bouillon. Add some sliced celery, carrots, onions, and garlic. The poultry seasonings of your choice—sparingly. Rice. A bay leaf. You will probably have to add more water midway. Oh, and you'll need a larger Pot.

"CORN SOUP" (CHIPOTLE CORN CHOWDER) *Serves 4*

■ **By Robby Millsap**

I make this soup for my kids and they go nuts for it. They call it "Corn Soup" and ask for it every week.

Ingredients:
½ russet potato, diced
½ onion, diced very small
½ teaspoon onion powder
½ cup water
1 pint chicken stock
4 ounces heavy cream
1 dried chipotle pepper, cut in half
½ teaspoon minced garlic
1 can corn, sauce drained
Kosher salt to taste
Black pepper to taste
White pepper to taste

Grated Cheddar cheese, for serving (optional)

Method:
Begin with the potato, onion, onion powder, and water. It just needs to simmer long enough for the potato to cook and the water to evaporate. Then add the other ingredients.

I puree the soup after cooking it into a nice corn chowder. Serve with freshly grated Cheddar cheese on top if you like.

JAMBALAYA SOUP

■ **By Aixa Serrano, Chicago**

Ingredients:
- 1½ cups uncooked rice
- 1 pound shrimp or crawfish
- 1 stick unsalted butter, melted
- 1 large onion, chopped
- 1 cup diced bell pepper
- 3 celery ribs, diced
- 2 teaspoons Cajun seasoning
- 2 cans beef broth
- 2 teaspoons black pepper
- 1 teaspoon chili powder
- 2 teaspoons garlic powder
- 1 to 2 teaspoons cayenne

Method:

Put all the ingredients, except the shrimp, in the Pot and cook on the regular cycle. Add andouille sausage if you like, but it should be sliced first and seared in a frying pan. Add shrimp for the last 5 minutes of cooking.

NONVEGETARIAN STEWS

CHICKEN ANDOUILLE *Serves 4*

■ **By Bob Auler, the sage of Urbana, on November 2, 2008 8:42 A.M.**

This chicken has a wonderful blend of tastes—not too hot, but a sweet, spicy flavor deep in the liquid.

Ingredients:

4 chicken thighs (use breasts if you must)

2 sliced andouille sausages (even the packaged ones in the wiener section)

About ½ cup 4-star balsamic vinegar (you need the good stuff . . . pop for it)

Maybe ¾ cup orange juice (don't start tasting yet—this changes flavors)

Maybe 1 teaspoon sea salt

1 bottle mushrooms (I use the fancy ones, but it doesn't matter)

½ red onion, sliced and diced

1 tomato, a little mushy, diced (doesn't matter if it's mushy, but saves a lost tomato)

2 tablespoons peach preserves

Method:

Put all the ingredients in the Pot and give it time, 30 to 40 minutes. You'll know from the aroma when it's done.

EBERT: From my favorite Libertarian! You indicate this is for a Crock-Pot. I wonder if it would work in a (large enough) rice Pot if you added the right amount of liquid—maybe just water, to not throw off the flavor.

MISS INA'S BEEF STEW FOR THE RICE COOKER *Makes 4 to 6 cups of soup*

■ By Ina New-Jones on November 15, 2008 6:40 P.M.

Ingredients:

- 1 pound beef stew meat (may substitute with other meats–chicken or oxtails)
- 1 can tomato sauce
- ¼ cup chopped onion
- ¼ cup chopped bell pepper
- 1 cup chopped celery
- ½ cup diced frozen or fresh carrots
- ½ cup frozen peas
- ½ cup diced potatoes
- ½ cup frozen or fresh lima beans
- 1 package Lipton onion soup
- 1 teaspoon minced garlic
- ½ teaspoon onion salt
- ½ cup water

Method:

Brown the stew meat in a skillet, then combine all the ingredients together in the rice cooker for approximately 45 minutes, or until the cooker turns off. Stir occasionally.

UNCLE ROGER: Miss Ina, why were we ordering out from Father & Son when you could have made this for us in less time than the pizza took to arrive? Can I put a little Worcestershire in my serving, please? You don't mean to tell me your boys would rather have pizza than their mom's stew made with beef, veggies, and love!

15

VEGETARIAN RECIPES

VEGETARIAN GRAINS

TANGY, STICKY SUSHI-STYLE RICE

■ By Devin Chalmers on November 2, 2008 6:18 A.M.

Method:

1. Rinse white short-grain rice carefully. The water should be clear, and long-grain rice is for Communists.
2. Add a little (maybe a third by volume) more water than rice. Let it soak for a good half hour or so.
3. Cook in the Pot.
4. While the Pot goes, prepare a solution of approximately 5 parts rice vinegar, 1 part sugar, and a bit of salt. Call it a third of a cup total for 2 to 3 cups of rice. Microwaves can help with this, or you can cleverly harness steam from the Pot to assist dissolution.
5. Remove the rice to a large, shallow bowl-like thing. Have a friend fan the rice while you drizzle the vinegar concoction and gently turn the rice. (Fanning helps with the stickiness.)

For extra fun:

1. Add (low-sodium? perhaps) soy sauce and wasabi for a cheap cheap cheap alternative to waiting in line at a sushi restaurant. All you really wanted was the soy sauce and wasabi, right?
2. Make rice balls! You can put things inside them. I suggest using a piece of plastic wrap to keep your hands clean if

you're making more than a few. Make a hole with your thumb to insert fillings—maybe something sweet, bits of pickle, anything.

3. For added points shape your rice ball into a fat triangle and wrap with seaweed. Eat while the nori is crispy.

4. Rice balls are notoriously hard to keep more than a day; they dry out in the fridge very quickly. I've had some limited luck microwaving them a bit.

MISS INA'S DOWN-HOME RICE PUDDING *Serves 4 to 6*

■ By Ina New-Jones on November 15, 2008 6:40 P.M.

Ingredients:
- 2 cups rice
- 3 cups water
- ½ stick unsalted butter
- 1 teaspoon ground cinnamon
- 1 teaspoon vanilla extract
- ½ teaspoon grated nutmeg
- ½ cup evaporated milk
- ¾ cup brown or granulated sugar

Method:
1. Combine all the ingredients in the rice cooker. The cooker will turn off when done.
2. Heat the oven to 350°F.
3. Pour the cooked rice into a greased baking dish; cook in the oven for 30 or 40 minutes.

UNCLE ROGER: Or three other people and me.

MEXICAN RICE *Serves 4*

■ **By jim in SF on January 2, 2009 3:03 P.M.**

Like in the restaurants, only with flavor.

Ingredients:

½ onion, chopped

Olive oil

3 cups rice

2 to 4 ounces tequila (taste first to make sure it's OK!)

Salt to taste

Ground cumin to taste

Ground cinnamon to taste

Dried oregano to taste

Ground cloves to taste

1 can tomatoes (in winter), preferably Mexican style with flavorings, or fresh skinned tomatoes

Method:

1. Sauté the chopped onion in the Pot with olive oil.
2. Add the rice and stir into the oil until well coated.
3. Add some tequila.
4. Add hot water to the 3-cup line; add salt to taste.
5. Add any or all of the cumin, cinnamon, oregano, and cloves.
6. Add the tomatoes.
7. Stir the Pot after the cooker finishes, let sit 10 minutes more, and serve.

OATMEAL IN A POT *Serves 4*

■ **By Jerry Roberts on January 7, 2009 9:37 A.M.**

Ingredients:

1⅓ cups rolled oats (not instant)

¾ cup water

2 cups apple juice

½ cup raisins (or fruit of your choice)

Method:

Add all the ingredients to the Pot. Cover and cook for 15 to 20 minutes (unless the cooker shuts off first). Stir only once during the cooking process to prevent sticking. Cover and let stand for 5 minutes.

I have been told that you have to spray the cooker first, but I haven't done it and the oatmeal has turned out fine.

COZY RICE SALAD

■ **By Jeanne Atkinson on January 7, 2009 12:01 P.M.**

Method:

Make a pot of rice. I prefer basmati. Place a layer of raw spinach and arugula at the bottom of your rice bowl. Pile on the rice. The heat from the rice will wilt the greens to perfection. Top with a sprinkle of toasted sesame oil and soy sauce. You can also add walnuts. Then get cozy on the couch and dig in.

EBERT'S TRUE GRITS!

Adapted from http://startcooking.com/blog/360/How-to-Make-Grits

Ingredients:

½ cup real stone-ground grits
2½ cups water, maybe a splash more
1 tablespoon butter
Dash of salt

Method:

1. Place all the ingredients in the Pot.
2. When the grits have boiled 60 seconds, switch to Hold and leave alone for 45 minutes.
3. If the grits are too firm, they needed a little more water or a little more boiling, or both. Experiment.

COLD RICE SALAD

■ **By Margo Howard**

Ingredients:

Cooked rice (refrigerated)
Chopped tomatoes
Chopped cukes
Raisins
Cashews
Fresh mint
Lemon juice and vinegar

Method:

You'll notice there are no amounts. This is because it was made by a great cook, Anne Peretz, who just . . . knew.

VEGETARIAN SOUPS

PUMPKIN SOUP

■ **By Rob Lindsay on November 3, 2008 2:22 P.M.**

I usually use a Dutch oven for this one, but it would probably work with a Pot as well. You might need to cut the recipe in half or adjust the cooking times, depending on the size of your Pot. (Note: Our recipe testers found the times suggested here worked fine with the Pot.)

Ingredients:
2 carrots, chopped
2 celery ribs, chopped
1 small (baseball-sized) onion, chopped
About 2 tablespoons butter
1 (29-ounce) can pumpkin
3 (14-ounce) cans vegetable broth
5 whole cloves
Skim milk, cream, or half-and-half
2 tablespoons honey
Salt and pepper

Method:
1. Sauté the carrots, celery, and onion with the butter in the bottom of the Pot for a few minutes.
2. Add the pumpkin, vegetable broth, and the cloves.
3. Simmer until the vegetables are tender. (I don't know how you "simmer" with the Pot, but I usually give it about 30 minutes on medium-low with the Dutch oven.)
4. Remove the cloves.
5. Puree the soup in batches in a blender, about 1½ cups at a time.
6. Add some skim milk, cream, or half-and-half (your choice), the honey, and salt and pepper to taste.
7. Drizzle a little milk or cream on top of the soup before serving.

GREEN SOUP *Serves 6*

■ By Anna Thomas

Green soup, the original, the elixir. If this one couldn't be made in the rice cooker, well, friends—the rice cooker and I would have to part ways.

The question that needed to be answered was, can we successfully brown some onions in the rice cooker? Yes, we can, is the happy answer, but we must remember that we are outwitting the appliance to do so. Roger likes to say, "The Pot *knows*." Well, in this case, we are telling it to do what it *does not know*.

Of course, it is easier to do on a conventional range, in a normal soup pot, caramelizing the onions in a regular skillet over a flame you can regulate—and it takes a little longer. But it is possible! So if you only have a rice cooker (you in the dorm room, you in the studio, etc., etc. . . . .) you are still in business.

Ingredients:

- 1 (8-ounce) bunch chard or spinach
- 1 (8-ounce) bunch kale
- 2 tablespoons extra-virgin olive oil, plus more for garnish
- 1 large yellow onion, chopped
- 1¼ teaspoons sea salt, more to taste
- 2 garlic cloves, chopped
- 3 tablespoons Arborio rice
- 3 cups water
- 3 cups vegetable broth, homemade or canned*
- 4 to 5 green onions, sliced
- ½ cup chopped fresh cilantro
- Pinch of cayenne
- 2 tablespoons fresh lemon juice, plus more to taste
- Freshly ground black pepper
- Crumbled fresh white cheese and homemade croutons, for garnish (optional)

Method:

Wash the greens thoroughly, trim off the tough kale stems, and slice the leaves.

Now the fun part—browning that onion. The rice cooker has only two settings: insanely high and barely warm. Put the 2 tablespoons olive oil into the Pot, plug in the Pot, and set it on insanely high (Cook); then, add the chopped onion and a big pinch of salt and cover the Pot. Every 5 minutes or so, lift the lid and give the onion a stir, and then cover again until the Pot switches itself to Keep Warm.

This is where you must *dominate the Pot*. Kick it back to Cook! I found that it will stay on Cook for about 3 minutes, several times in a row. When it absolutely refuses to go back to Cook (thinks it's done, silly thing), let it rest on Keep Warm for a few minutes. Then go to Cook again, adding the chopped garlic this time, and keep at it until you have onion that is soft and brown. All this will probably take a total of about 40 minutes. The onion will not be as evenly and gently caramelized as it might be in a pan over a carefully adjusted medium-low flame—but it'll be good!

Add the rice, water, vegetable broth, and a teaspoon of sea salt to the onion and garlic in the Pot. Cover and set on Cook. As soon as the liquid is simmering, which shouldn't take longer than about 5 minutes, start piling in the prepared greens, the green onions, and the cilantro. It will look like too much—it's not. Push the greens down gently with a spoon until you can replace the lid. Cook for half an hour.

Unplug the Pot, and puree the soup carefully with an immersion blender. Alternately, allow the soup to cool a little and puree it in a normal blender, in batches, then return to the Pot.

Add the cayenne and the lemon juice, grind in some black pepper, and stir. Now use your taste buds—correct the seasoning to your taste with a drop more lemon juice, another pinch of salt, or even a bit more pepper. Just add the right amount, honey, until you have the balance you like.

I always finish this soup in the bowl with my all-time favorite garnish—a thin drizzle of fruity olive oil. This is not a decoration, but an essential part of the soup. The taste of the fresh, unheated oil is entirely different from the taste of cooked oil, and I deliberately use a modest amount of oil in the cooking process so that I can add some fresh oil at the end.

Other garnishes can be added. Crumbled white cheese is a natural—either cotija, feta, or queso fresco. Homemade croutons are also great in this soup.

*See the first chapter in *Love Soup* for everything you need to know about making delicious vegetable broth—it's dead easy, but you need a stockpot. So unless you have some Paul Bunyan version of a rice cooker, we're not talking about *that Pot*. Do what I do when I don't have homemade broth on hand: Use Swanson's canned vegetable broth. It's the only commercial broth I've tried that tastes any good. Forget about those fancy, expensive boxes at the health food store, and don't even think about using a bouillon cube or a powder—you will have your soup license revoked.

SMOKEY SPLIT PEA SOUP *Serves 6 to 8*

■ By Anna Thomas

This is an adaptation of the Old-Fashioned Split Pea Soup in my book *Love Soup*. It is very simple to make, and thus bends easily to the demands of the Pot. Only a little bit of Pot wrangling is involved.

I made a couple of subtle changes in this recipe, adding a bit of olive oil at the start and seasoning with a smoked hot paprika—I have to admit, it's even better now.

Ingredients:

- 1 large yellow onion, chopped
- 2 tablespoons extra-virgin olive oil, plus more for garnish
- 3 celery ribs, chopped
- 3 to 4 carrots, chopped
- 1 pound green split peas, rinsed
- 8 cups water
- 1 bay leaf
- 2 teaspoons chopped fresh thyme, or 1 teaspoon dried thyme
- ¼ teaspoon smoked hot paprika, such as Pimentón de la Vera
- ¼ cup finely chopped fresh flat-leaf parsley
- 1½ teaspoons sea salt
- 2 cups light vegetable broth, homemade or canned*
- Freshly ground black pepper
- Homemade croutons (optional)

Method:

Combine the onion and the olive oil in the Pot. Set the Pot to Cook and cover it. Every 5 minutes or so, lift the cover and give the onion a stir. Continue doing this for 15 to 20 minutes, or until the Pot switches itself to Keep Warm. The onion should be translucent and at least starting to have some golden color. Add the celery and carrots, wait a moment, then defy the Pot and switch it back to Cook.

Cook the vegetables, covered, stirring every few minutes, until the Pot will not allow you to do so any longer—or 15 more minutes, whichever comes first.

Add the split peas, water, bay leaf, thyme, and paprika. Cover the Pot and flip it back to Cook—it will stay there this time. Set your timer for an hour. After an hour, the split peas should be tender and breaking apart. Add the parsley, salt, and the broth, and grind in some black pepper. Cover the Pot and cook for another 20 minutes. Everything should be very soft.

Remove the bay leaf. Puree the soup in the Pot with an immersion blender, or do it the old-fashioned way in a stand-up blender, in batches. Make it velvety smooth. Now try a spoonful and use those taste buds, honey. Correct the seasoning with another pinch of salt, a little more spicy paprika, or a bit more pepper. You'll know when it's just right.

Serve the soup steaming hot, with another swirl of olive oil in each bowl—and crunchy whole-grain croutons if you've got them.

*OK, I've said it before, but here it is again. No bouillon cubes! No powders! If you need to use a canned broth, go ahead, but use a good-tasting one. My backup cans are Swanson's—from the supermarket, not the health food store. Easy.

SUMMER TOMATO AND BASIL SOUP WITH FARRO *Serves 6 to 7*

■ By Anna Thomas

This is a simple, rustic tomato soup—it's really just an easy tomato sauce with some broth and farro added. But simple does not mean ordinary! It's the pure taste of summer, the sweetness and tang of real tomatoes. Only make this soup when delicious, vine-ripened tomatoes are in plentiful supply.

The usual cautions apply in adapting this to the rice cooker: Sautéing the onion and garlic is a bit of a power struggle between you and the gadget, but you can easily win. And you might have to adjust the amount of liquid at the end, as the Pot only boils or stands still, and some liquid will go up in steam. But when I made this soup in the Pot, the result was delicious—good tomatoes overcome all obstacles.

Note:

I have often made this soup with orzo or with rice, but once I tried farro, there was no turning back. Farro is an ancient form of wheat, the stuff that kept the Roman legions going. And they didn't even have a rice cooker. The semipeeled grain, which looks, not surprisingly, like wheat berries, cooks up in 25 to 30 minutes, the whole grain in about 45 minutes. Farro can be bought in better Italian groceries, well-stocked natural foods stores, and online. If you don't want to get farro, go ahead and use half a cup of orzo or some cooked rice.

Ingredients:

- 3½ pounds vine-ripe tomatoes
- 2 tablespoons extra-virgin olive oil, plus more for garnish
- 1 small yellow onion, chopped
- 1½ teaspoons sea salt, more to taste
- 4 garlic cloves, finely chopped
- ½ cup chopped or torn fresh basil leaves
- 4½ cups vegetable broth, homemade or canned*
- 1¼ cups cooked farro
- Freshly ground black pepper
- Freshly grated Parmigiano-Reggiano (optional)

Method:

First, you must peel the tomatoes. Half-fill the Pot with water and bring it to a boil. Cut shallow crosses in the tomatoes with a sharp knife and scald them in the boiling water for about 45 seconds, a minute at the most. Lift them out with a slotted spoon, rinse them with cold water, and slip off their skins. Toss the water and wipe the Pot clean.

Chop the tomatoes coarsely by hand, or process them briefly in a blender so that they are rough and chunky, but not yet a puree. Save all the juice!

Put 2 tablespoons of olive oil into the clean Pot, and set it on Cook. Add the onion and a pinch of salt and cover the Pot. Check the progress of the onion every 5 minutes or so, lifting the lid and giving it a quick stir. If the infernal gadget switches itself to Keep Warm, flip it back to Cook. If it refuses to stay there, wait a couple of minutes, then show it who's boss.

After about 20 minutes, your onion should be getting a nice golden color, flecked with brown. Add the garlic, stir, and cook for another 3 or 4 minutes. Add the tomatoes with their juice, the basil, and a teaspoon of salt, and cover the Pot. Set your timer for 30 minutes.

Add the vegetable broth (you may not need all of the 4½ cups) and the cooked farro, cover, and set the timer for another 15 minutes. (If you are adding uncooked orzo instead of cooked farro, adjust the broth to accommodate that—orzo should be cooked within the 15 minutes, but it will absorb a bit more liquid.)

Switch the setting to Keep Warm, and grind in plenty of black pepper. Taste the soup and adjust the seasoning with a bit more sea salt if needed. If it seems too thick—you know what to do.

Drizzle a generous loop of your best olive oil on top of each steaming bowl of this soup, and pass the grated Parmigiano.

*If you are using canned broth, use a good one—Swanson's is the one I use. I can't stomach any of the others I have tried. Don't you dare use a bouillon cube or a powder. I don't care what Roger says. Who are you going to believe about cooking, him or me?

METRIC CONVERSIONS AND EQUIVALENTS

METRIC CONVERSION FORMULAS

To Convert	Multiply
Ounces to grams	Ounces by 28.35
Pounds to kilograms	Pounds by .454
Teaspoons to milliliters	Teaspoons by 4.93
Tablespoons to milliliters	Tablespoons by 14.79
Fluid ounces to milliliters	Fluid ounces by 29.57
Cups to milliliters	Cups by 236.59
Cups to liters	Cups by .236
Pints to liters	Pints by .473
Quarts to liters	Quarts by .946
Gallons to liters	Gallons by 3.785
Inches to centimeters	Inches by 2.54

APPROXIMATE METRIC EQUIVALENTS

Volume

¼ teaspoon	1 milliliter
½ teaspoon	2.5 milliliters
¾ teaspoon	4 milliliters
1 teaspoon	5 milliliters
2 teaspoons	10 milliliters
1 tablespoon (½ fluid ounce)	15 milliliters
¼ cup	60 milliliters
⅓ cup	80 milliliters
½ cup (4 fluid ounces)	120 milliliters
⅔ cup	160 milliliters
¾ cup	180 milliliters
1 cup (8 fluid ounces)	240 milliliters
2 cups (1 pint)	460 milliliters
3 cups	700 milliliters
4 cups (1 quart)	.95 liter
1 quart plus ¼ cup	1 liter
4 quarts (1 gallon)	3.8 liters

Weight

¼ ounce	7 grams
½ ounce	14 grams
¾ ounce	21 grams
1 ounce	28 grams
2 ounces	57 grams
3 ounces	85 grams
4 ounces (¼ pound)	113 grams
5 ounces	142 grams
6 ounces	170 grams
7 ounces	198 grams
8 ounces (½ pound)	227 grams
16 ounces (1 pound)	454 grams
35.25 ounces (2.2 pounds)	1 kilogram

Length

¼ inch	6 millimeters
½ inch	1¼ centimeters
1 inch	2½ centimeters
2 inches	5 centimeters
6 inches	15¼ centimeters
12 inches (1 foot)	30 centimeters

OVEN TEMPERATURES

To convert Fahrenheit to Celsius, subtract 32 from Fahrenheit, multiply the result by 5, then divide by 9.

Description	Fahrenheit	Celsius	British Gas Mark
Very cool	200°	95°	0
Very cool	225°	110°	¼
Very cool	250°	120°	½
Cool	275°	135°	1
Cool	300°	150°	2
Warm	325°	165°	3
Moderate	350°	175°	4
Moderately hot	375°	190°	5
Fairly hot	400°	200°	6
Hot	425°	220°	7
Very hot	450°	230°	8
Very hot	475°	245°	9

Common Ingredients and Their Approximate Equivalents

1 cup uncooked rice = 225 grams

1 cup all-purpose flour = 140 grams

1 stick butter (4 ounces • ½ cup • 8 tablespoons) = 110 grams

1 cup butter (8 ounces • 2 sticks • 16 tablespoons) = 220 grams

1 cup brown sugar, firmly packed = 225 grams

1 cup granulated sugar = 200 grams

Information compiled from *Recipes into Type* by Joan Whitman and Dolores Simon (Newton, MA: Biscuit Books, 2000); *The New Food Lover's Companion* by Sharon Tyler Herbst (Hauppauge, NY: Barron's, 1995); and *Rosemary Brown's Big Kitchen Instruction Book* (Kansas City, MO: Andrews McMeel, 1998).

INDEX